DATE DUE

A 675			
E			
OCT 27 1980			
GAYLORD			PRINTED IN U.S A.

FAMOUS MEN OF SCIENCE

FAMOUS MEN
OF SCIENCE

BY SARAH K. BOLTON

Revised by Barbara Lovett Cline

THOMAS Y. CROWELL COMPANY · NEW YORK

The following publishers have kindly given their permission
to reprint copyrighted material:

Harper & Brothers, for excerpts from ATOMS AND PEOPLE by
Ralph Lapp.
The University of Chicago Press, for excerpts from ATOMS
IN THE FAMILY by Laura Fermi. Copyright 1954 by The
University of Chicago.

CONTENTS

FAMOUS MEN OF SCIENCE

CHAPTER I

Nicolaus Copernicus

Carlyle once remarked that the history of the world is the history of its great men. It might be said with equal truth that the history of astronomy is a record of the lives of the great astronomers.

Just who was the first astronomer is not known for certain. This distinction, however, is frequently credited to Hipparchus, who was born about 170 B.C. He made a catalogue of the positions of the stars and was spoken of by Ptolemy, some two hundred years later, as a "most truth-loving and labor-saving man."

But whoever was the first astronomer, it is certain that early in his history man began to study the stars. Some knowledge of astronomy was needed in order to fix dates for fasts and festivals—events of paramount importance in ancient and medieval times.

It is probable that early scientists studied the heavens merely as a side line. Thus Aristotle, who exercised a profound influence in this branch of learning, was both an all-round scientist and a philosopher. Claudius Ptolemy, one of the most famous of the ancient astronomers, who lived in Egypt in the second century, was a mathematician and geographer as well. He held that the earth was the immovable center of the universe, round which revolved, in order, the moon, Mercury, Venus, the sun, Mars, Jupiter, Saturn, and the stars. This theory was so entwined with matters of the Church and Scriptures that it remained absolutely unquestioned for fourteen hundred years. When Nicolaus Copernicus, himself many things besides an astronomer, became satisfied that the theory was false, he hesitated to denounce it, knowing that charges of heresy would be brought against him.

The proclamation and proof of his discovery ushered into the world a new era of philosophical belief. Today to be the Copernicus of any movement means to show honesty and freedom of thought—as did the old monk who lived a life of solitude in the monastery gardens at Frauenburg over four centuries ago.

Nicolaus Copernicus was born in the town of Torun, on the Prussian frontier, February 19, 1473. His father was a successful tradesman; his mother was a sister of Lucas Watzelrode, Bishop of Ermeland—a relationship which proved helpful to the young Copernicus.

Little is known of Copernicus' early life, beyond the fact that he was a serious youth who was particularly interested in Latin and Greek. His education was carried on at home until he was able to enter the University of Cracow, where he planned to study medicine. While at the university, he developed aptitudes for mathematics, natural philosophy, and draftsmanship.

After he graduated from Cracow in both arts and medicine, Copernicus set himself up in Rome as a mathematician and astronomer. He was soon so well and favorably known that he was offered the chair of mathematics in the University of Rome. He did not occupy this position long, however. His uncle, the Bishop of Ermeland, had kept an eye on the young man's progress, which pleased him. Wanting Copernicus to be identified with his Prussian homeland, his uncle offered him the canonry of the cathedral at Frauenburg.

Copernicus believed that he needed further preparation for his new position and entered the medical department of the University of Padua. He remained there until 1505, when he was stationed at the palace of Heilsberg for additional preliminary service as the Bishop's private physician. Here he found his life complicated by the resentment of envious people over his "pull" with the Bishop. But this animosity did not last, and on his uncle's death Copernicus found himself in unquestioned possession of the canonry. Here he fell into a daily round which was characteristic of this man of precision. Carefully dividing his time into thirds, he gave his day (1) to devotional exercises and diligent performance of his religious duties; (2) to charitably tending the poor who were in need of medical care; (3) to the pursuit of his hobby—the study of astronomy and philosophical meditation upon it.

Copernicus wielded considerable influence among his parishioners, and was frequently called upon for advice on affairs of state. When wars upset financial standards and the Diet could not satisfactorily settle the money question, a committee of senators was appointed to investigate. Unable to solve the problem, the committee finally appealed to Copernicus. He set himself at once to the gigantic task, and presently evolved a plan for reducing to a definite standard the various moneys then in circulation in the provinces of the kingdom. At the same time he wrote a valuable circular on the general subject of money. His pamphlet was published, and his plan immediately adopted by the senate, who inserted it in the public Acts.

One of the chief instruments in the modern observatory is a transit telescope. It is mounted so that it can swing only on the plane of the meridian, and therefore, sooner or later in the course of every twenty-four hours, all stars must cross its path. The time of their crossing is of particular importance in determining astronomical data. Copernicus had no transit instrument; in fact, he had no notion whatever of a telescope of any kind, for this instrument was not invented until more than seventy-five years after his death. But Copernicus solved problems in his own way: he had slits cut in the walls of his observation room. By placing himself suitably, he could note the transit of the stars across a prescribed meridian. Also, by means of a quadrant of his own making, he succeeded in measuring the altitude of various stars above the horizon.

From the very first, Copernicus was interested in the movement of the planets, and the tables which he compiled were the best of his times. They remained in use long after he died. He made special studies of the planet Mars and, curious about the variable brightness and magnitude of this planet, he turned to Ptolemy's theory for an explanation. According to this theory, the earth was stationary, and the planets, sun, moon, and stars, while not revolving directly around it, yet revolved around imaginary points which in turn revolved about the earth in a circular path known as the deferent circle. It was a complex system and few people understood it.

The more Copernicus thought about the Ptolemaic system, the less satisfied he became. Was it possible that nature, which as a rule behaved in the simplest way, moved in this ponderous scheme of circles? If he had not been so deeply religious, Copernicus might have felt—as Alphonso X, King of Castile, said of himself—that he "could have given some useful hints at the Creation!"

Instead, his dissatisfaction only made him more doubtful, and he turned to the records of science for support in what he considered must be the real facts of the case: that *the sun* and not the earth was the center of our solar system, and that it was the rotation of the earth on its axis which caused day and night, and the revolution of the earth about the sun which caused the change of the seasons. He soon found that he was not the first to have had such ideas. Two thousand years before, Pythagoras, a Greek philosopher, had voiced the opinion that the sun was the center of the planetary system, and one of his followers, Aristarchus, who lived some four hundred years before Ptolemy, had suggested the rotation of the earth to account for the diurnal motion of the heavens. Both, however, had been overruled by Aristotle and Ptolemy, whose own strong beliefs were later backed by the Roman Church. It was preposterous, Ptolemy had argued, to think of the earth in rotation. If such were the case, the rush of atmosphere would sweep men off the surface. Copernicus answered this argument in his own mind by saying that the inhabitants would be carried by the earth in the same manner as a man carries his overcoat. Besides, would it not be much simpler for the earth, along with the other planets, to revolve around the sun, in an orbit between Venus and Mars, than for the whole system of intricate circles to revolve about the earth? If his supposition were correct, he added, Venus and Mercury should exhibit phases like the moon. But this point was not proved until after Galileo, first to observe the heavens with a telescope, had clinched the Copernican theory beyond a doubt.

How long Copernicus was convinced of his theory before he communicated it to others is a matter of some conjecture. He found difficulty in breaking away from the "circle worship" of the old philosophers. Besides, who was he to voice an opinion so contrary to the Church and all established belief? Some way, however, a hint leaked out, and scientists, flocking to Frauenburg to learn the truth, went away fully satisfied that Copernicus was right.

But for many years the old monk could not be persuaded to put his theory into print for the benefit of the world. His loyalty to the Church was strong and his disposition retiring. He disliked argument and controversy, and had small heart for facing all the stigma which would be attached to him for heresy. Besides, though he was entirely sure of the facts of the case, a good deal was based on supposition; he could not prove his theory, much less make a satisfactory diagram of the sun and the planetary system.

His ideas were confused because he believed in epicycles (the theory that the planets revolved in smaller circles, and these circles, in turn, revolved about a central body), and he could not give up Ptolemy's idea of a deferent circle. It remained for Kepler in the next century to make a clean sweep of the complicated system of circles and substitute for it the simple ellipse.

Copernicus wrote down his ideas, but for thirteen years the manuscript remained unpublished. Finally he became too frail and old to undertake its publication himself. He gave the task to Rheticus, one of his students, who ably edited the work, which was given the title, *The Revolution of the Celestial Orbs.* But while the first copy was on its way to Copernicus, he suffered a paralytic stroke. The book reached him only a few hours before his death, at the age of seventy.

Copernicus was now beyond the power of the Church, but he had left behind in his book a masterly plea in the shape of a "dedicatory note" to Pope Paul III:

If there be some who, though ignorant of all mathematics, take upon them to judge of these, and dare to reprove this work, because of some passage of Scripture, which they have miserably warped to their purpose, I regard them not, and even despise their rash judgment. . . . What I have done in this matter, I submit principally to your holiness, and then to the judgment of all learned mathematicians. And that I may not seem to promise your Holiness more concerning the utility of this work than I am able to perform, I pass now to the work itself.

Judged by modern standards, Copernicus' work contained "much of error, unsound reasoning, and happy conjecture." It remained for Kepler, Galileo, and Newton to rectify the blunders and mature the general theory. The great achievement of Copernicus was that he discovered the proper place of the earth in the cosmic scheme. Although others before him had believed that the sun was the center of the solar system, this was of no particular importance, since they had failed to establish their belief. In an age when the Church enforced its creed with iron rigidity, Copernicus dared to differ and to record his convictions. Eventually, although not for many years, "Aristotle worship," which had impeded scientific progress for many centuries, was effectively broken up; the world emerged into a new scientific era.

Copernicus was buried in the cathedral at Frauenburg. Little attention was paid to his great discovery until thirty years later, when a memorial was erected to his memory.

Copernicus was a man of many talents, among them painting, which he did with considerable skill. In his early days, he painted a half-length portrait of himself, which later fell into the hands of Tycho Brahe, the poet and astronomer, who placed it in his museum above the following eulogy:

Phoebus no more his bounding Coursers drives
Sublime in Air; the task to Earth he gives.
Amidst the world enthron'd he sits in State,
And bids the Heav'ns obey the Laws of Fate;
Yet thro' all Nature is his Aid the same,
And changing Seasons still his Guidance claim.
Erratic Stars have now their Courses known,
By this rare System of the station'd Sun;
They stand, go retrograde, are swift, or slow,
Just as the Earth directs them what to do.

The great Copernicus (the Man behold),
This heavy Orb in rapid Motion roll'd.
But why, you'll say, was not his Wit portray'd?
But that is partly in the Heav'n display'd,
Partly in Earth; for neither can confine
The boundless Searches of his daring Mind.
Again you'll say—But half his Figure's shown,
A Man so worthy to be wholly known.
True; yet 'tis he who bore the Earth entire
Thro' Space immense around the Solar Fire:
The spacious Earth in vain would hold the Man
Who measures Heaven with his ample Span.

CHAPTER 2

Galileo Galilei

"The same memorable day is marked by the setting of one of the most brilliant stars in the firmament of art and the rising of another in the sphere of science, which was to enlighten the world with beams of equal splendor. On the 18th of February, 1564, Michael Angelo Buonarotti closed his eyes at Rome, and Galileo Galilei first saw the light at Pisa."

Thus wrote Karl von Gebler, in his life of Galileo. Some other authorities place Galileo's birth on February 15.

Galileo was the oldest in a family of five children born to Vincenzo Galilei, a Florentine noble, and Giulia Ammanati, who also belonged to an ancient family. Vincenzo wrote learnedly about music, and taught his boy to play on the lute and the organ. But he was poor and life was a struggle, so Vincenzo decided to place his son where he could earn a comfortable living. Since music did not bring money, he decided that Galileo should become a dealer in cloth—a necessity of life, rather than a luxury.

But Galileo soon showed great skill in music, as well as marked aptitudes for drawing, poetry, and mechanics. It soon became evident that he would never be satisfied to spend his life trading in wool.

He must be educated, but how? The family had moved from Pisa, where there were excellent schools, to Florence. They were determined that Galileo should ultimately return to Pisa for study, and they practiced the strictest economy to pay for his preparation. He made rapid progress in Latin and Greek, and at seventeen was ready to leave Florence and enter the university in Pisa.

For what profession should he study? Not what best suited his tastes, but that in which his father thought he could make the most money—medicine.

At college, Galileo became an ardent student of philosophy, and because he dared to think for himself, and did not always agree with the teachings of Aristotle, which were universally regarded as the only truth, he was called "the wrangler." Until he was twenty, he knew little more than the rudiments of mathematics, because his father thought it a waste of time for a man who was to become a physician.

While Galileo was studying medicine in Pisa, boarding with a relative, the court of Tuscany came to the city for a few months. Among the attendants was Ostilio Ricci, a distinguished mathematician, and Governor of the Pages of the Grand Ducal Court. He was a friend of the Galilei family, and was pleased to see Galileo. When Ricci taught Euclid, the medical student would stand shyly at the schoolroom door and listen with intense interest. Soon he began to study mathematics secretly, then begged Ricci to teach him. Ricci consented—until Galileo's father forbade it on the grounds that Euclid interfered with medicine.

Meanwhile, Galileo, who was then nineteen, had dreamily watched a bronze lamp swinging from an arch in Pisa Cathedral while he knelt at prayers. The oscillations were at first quite long, but as they grew shorter and shorter, Galileo observed that they were all performed in the same time, measuring the time by feeling his pulse. It occurred to him that an instrument could be constructed which would mark the rate and variation of the pulse. He began to experiment and soon invented the pulsilogium, a pendulum which was quickly put into use by physicians. The pendulum was not applied to clocks till a half-century later, but its invention attracted the attention of all scientists.

After Galileo had studied for four years at Pisa, Vincenzo Galilei appealed to the reigning Grand Duke, Ferdinand de' Medici, to grant to his son one of the forty free places founded for poor students. The request was denied, and Galileo, unable to pay for his doctor's degree, was forced to leave the university without it.

He went back to his home in Florence to study the

works of Archimedes, whom he called his "master," to write his first essay on his Hydrostatic Balance, and to earn a considerable reputation in geometrical and mechanical speculations. His father had now given up all hope of Galileo's ever making a fortune in the practice of medicine.

When Galileo was twenty-four, Marquis Guidubaldo, a well-known mathematician, wrote to him suggesting that he study the position of the center of gravity in solid bodies. Galileo wrote a valuable essay on the subject—an essay which waited fifty years for publication.

Through the influence of the marquis, Galileo was brought to the notice of Ferdinand I, reigning Grand Duke, who appointed him to the mathematical professorship at Pisa. This was a great honor for a young man of twenty-six, who had been too poor to take his degree. The salary was small, less than a hundred dollars a year, but he earned additional income by practicing medicine, giving lectures on Dante and other literary subjects, and tutoring private pupils.

The professors at Pisa, with the single exception of Jacopo Mazzoni, in the chair of philosophy, were opposed to the newcomer. They were all disciples of Aristotle, and Galileo in his student days had dared to oppose the great Grecian.

One of the best-known stories about Galileo, that he dropped different weights from the top of the Leaning Tower of Pisa and observed that they took the same time to reach the ground, probably is not true. There is evidence that he relied far more on mathematics and deductive reasoning than on experiment. However, at some time he did make a crude experiment to prove his law of falling bodies and disprove the two-thousand-year-old law of Aristotle, that the speed of falling bodies depends on their weight. Scientists and learned men were astonished. If Aristotle could be wrong in one thing, he might be wrong in others. Galileo became a controversial figure.

The feeling against him grew so strong that after three years at Pisa he resigned. Through his friend, the Marquis Guidubaldo, Galileo obtained the mathematical professorship at Padua. He was now twenty-nine, and becoming widely known throughout Italy. His father had just died. Now Galileo's mother and four sisters and brothers depended solely on him for support.

Padua gave Galileo a cordial welcome. Vincenzo Pinelli, a nobleman who owned a library of eighty thousand volumes, mentioned Galileo as a man worth cultivating to Tycho Brahe, the great Danish astronomer. The Dane was cautious about his own reputation, however. He did not write Galileo until eight years later and died the following year.

But John Kepler, an associate of Tycho Brahe, sent Galileo his new book on astronomy. In a letter of thanks to Kepler, Galileo wrote:

Many years ago I became a convert to the opinions of Copernicus, and by that theory have succeeded in fully explaining many phenomena which on the contrary hypothesis are altogether inexplicable. I have drawn up many arguments and compilations of the opposite opinions, which, however, I have not hitherto dared to publish, fearful of meeting the same fate as our master Copernicus, who, although he has earned for himself immortal fame amongst the few, yet amongst the greater number appears as only worthy of hooting and derision; so great is the number of fools.

Like Galileo, John Kepler had money troubles all his life. His childhood was spent in the little beer-shop of his wretchedly poor father. At six he had a severe attack of smallpox, and after that his sight was weak. He was put to the plow to earn his living, but his delicate body could not do the work. At last, through charity, he became a theological student at Tübingen.

Fortunately for science, he heard some lectures given by Michael Möstlen, a famous mathematician and astronomer. A new world opened to Kepler. At twenty-two he became professor of mathematics at Grätz, in Austria. But he was soon driven away from this Catholic stronghold on account of his Protestant faith. Tycho Brahe heard of his difficulties, and made him his assistant at Prague, with the assurance of a regular salary.

This seemed regal splendor to the poor astronomer, but his happiness did not last long. His children died, his wife became insane and died also. His salary could not be paid because of the religious wars that disrupted Germany. Kepler wrote almanacs, took private pupils, and tried in every possible way to support his second wife and children. In the meantime, he continued his astronomical research year after year—and discovered his three great laws. The mathematical calculations for the first law, that the planets move in elliptical orbits around the sun, filled seven hundred pages. Seventeen years of research went into his third great law: "The squares of the periodic times of the planets are proportioned to the cubes of their mean distances from the sun."

When Kepler's book, *Harmonies of the World,* which contained his third law, was published, he said, "I have written my book. It will be read; whether in the present age or by posterity matters little. It can wait for its readers."

In a last fruitless attempt to recover twenty-nine thousand florins owed him by the government, worn out with want and disappointment, Kepler fell ill and died in Ratisbon, Bavaria, leaving thirty-three published works, twenty-two volumes in manuscript, and his family in the direst poverty. Such was the man who admired Galileo in his youth, and ranks with him in scientific stature.

At Padua, Galileo attracted great numbers to his classes. Often a thousand gathered to hear him lecture; when the hall was too cramped, he spoke to the people in the open air. He was above middle height and well proportioned; his temperament was cheerful; he was often witty and enthusiastic. His education was so extensive that he could repeat by heart much of the works of Virgil, Ovid, Horace, and Seneca, but in spite of his accomplishments, he was modest and unassuming, saying that he never met a man so ignorant but that something might be learned from him.

Galileo worked constantly. He wrote treatises on fortifications, on mechanics, on gnomonics (the science of telling time by means of shadows), on the laws of motion, on the celestial sphere. These articles were copied by his pupils and distributed by them throughout Europe. He took a workman into his family and superintended him in the construction of a compass that he had invented and a thermoscope, or heat indicator, a forerunner of the thermometer. This was made with a "glass bottle about the size of a hen's egg, the neck of which was two palms long, and as narrow as a straw. Having well heated the bulb in his hands, he placed its mouth in a vessel containing a little water, and withdrawing the heat of his hand from the bulb, instantly the water rose in the neck, more than a palm above the water in the vessel."

During his first six years at Padua, Galileo's salary was almost tripled, but he never had enough money. His sister, Virginia, had married before his father's death, but the promised dowry had never been paid. Now Benedetto, the brother-in-law, demanded payment. Galileo's mother was worried. She wrote to him:

If you carry into effect your intention of coming here next month, I shall be rejoiced, only you must not come

unprovided with funds, for I see that Benedetto is determined to have his own, that is to say, what you promised
him; and he threatens loudly that he will have you arrested
the instant you arrive here. And as I hear you bound your-
self to pay, he would have the power to arrest you, and
he is just the man to do it. So I warn you, for it would
grieve me much if anything of the kind were to happen.

Livia, another sister, had become engaged to a
Pisan gentleman, with the promise of a dowry of eighteen hundred ducats, eight hundred of which must be
paid down. Before he could make the payment, Galileo
had to borrow six hundred ducats.

Besides these sisters, Galileo had a lazy brother to
provide for, Michelangelo by name, a young man of
some musical talent, elegant manners, and not much
else. Galileo secured a place for him with a Polish
prince, and spent two hundred crowns to get him ready
for the new position. But Michelangelo soon returned,
and another place had to be found for him, this time at
the court of the Duke of Bavaria.

While in Bavaria, instead of helping to pay his
sister's dowry as he had promised, Michelangelo married, had an extravagant wedding feast, and then wrote
to his hard-working brother: "I know that you will say
that I should have waited, and thought of our sisters
before taking a wife. But, good heavens! the idea of
toiling all one's life just to put by a few farthings to
give one's sisters! This yoke would be indeed too heavy

and bitter; for I am more than certain that in thirty years I should not have saved enough to cover this debt."

In spite of the constant pressure upon him for money, Galileo kept steadily on in his absorbing studies. In 1609, he constructed a telescope. It is true that Hans Lippershey, of Holland, had invented a spyglass, and presented it to Prince Maurice, so that the principle was understood; but nobody gave it practical application till Galileo, having heard of the glass, began to reflect how an instrument could be made to bring distant objects nearer. At either end of a lead tube he fixed a glass lens, one concave (the eyepiece) and the other convex (the object glass). Whatever he viewed through this telescope appeared three times nearer and nine times larger. A few days later Galileo hastened with his lead tube to Venice, to exhibit it to the Doge and the Senate. In a letter to a friend he described what happened:

Many gentlemen and senators, even the oldest, have ascended at various times the highest bell-towers in Venice, to spy out ships at sea making sail for the mouth of the harbor, and have seen them clearly though without my telescope they would have been invisible for more than two hours. The effect of this instrument is to show an object at a distance of, say, fifty miles, as if it were but five miles off.

Perceiving of what great utility such an instrument would prove in naval and military operations, and seeing that His Serenity greatly desired to possess it, I resolved four days ago to go to the palace and present it to the Doge as a free gift. And on quitting the presence-chamber, I was commanded to bide a while in the hall of the senate, whereunto, after a little, the Illustrissimo Prioli, who is Procurator and one of the Riformatori of the University, came forth to me from the presence-chamber, and, taking me by the hand, said that "the Senate, knowing the manner in which I had served it for seventeen years at Padua, and being sensible of my courtesy in making it a present of my telescope, had immediately ordered the illustrious Riformatori to elect me (with my good will) to the professorship for life, with a stipend of one thousand florins yearly."

On his return to Padua, Galileo began to study the heavens. He found that the surface of the moon was mountainous; that the Milky Way was composed of an immense number of stars "planted together in clusters"; that Orion, instead of being made up of seven heavenly bodies, had over five hundred stars; and that the Pleiades were not seven, but thirty-six. In January, 1610, he discovered the four large moons of Jupiter, and observed that they revolved around it. During the same year, he discovered the ring of Saturn, the phases of Venus, and the sunspots.

Florence and Padua were in a blaze of excitement. These new discoveries seemed to prove that the earth was not the center of the universe, and that Copernicus had been right when he declared the sun to be the center. Galileo's observations were profoundly upsetting, for people believed, as had Aristotle, that the stars and planets they saw in the heavens *were* heavenly, that each was guided by a "special intelligence" and made of perfect material which could move only in perfect circles around a stationary earth. Now Galileo was saying that the celestial bodies obeyed the same physical laws that the earth obeyed, that they were as imperfect and as changeable as the earth. It was almost as if someone had questioned the existence of heaven.

Opposition to Galileo was bitter, widespread, and took some curious forms. Some of the Aristotelians declared that the telescope of Galileo showed things that did not exist. One of them wrote:

It is ridiculous that four planets [Jupiter's moons] are chasing each other around a large planet.

It is angels who make Saturn, Jupiter, the sun, etc. turn round. If the earth revolves, it must also have an angel in the center to set it in motion; for if only devils live there, it would, therefore, be a devil who would impart motion to the earth.

The planets, the sun, the fixed stars, all belong to one species; namely, that of stars—they, therefore, all move, or all stand still.

It seems, therefore, to be a grievous wrong to place the earth, which is a sink of impurity, among the heavenly bodies, which are pure and divine things.

Libri, one of the Pisan professors, spoke of the new discoveries as "celestial trifles." When he died, Galileo remarked, "Libri did not choose to see my celestial trifles while he was on earth; perhaps he will, now he is gone to heaven."

Now Galileo longed for freedom from teaching,

so that he could devote more time to study and writing. He had planned, he said,

two books on the system of the universe: an immense work (*concetto,* "idea") full of philosophy, astronomy, and geometry; three books on local motion, a science entirely new . . . three books on mechanics, two on the demonstration of its first principles, and one of problems; and though this is a subject which has already been treated by various writers, yet all which has been written hitherto neither in quantity nor otherwise is the quarter of what I am writing on it. I have also various treatises on natural subjects, on sound and speech, on sight and colors, on the tide, on the composition of continuous quantity, on the motion of animals, and others; besides, I have also an idea of writing some books on the military art, giving not only a model of a soldier, but teaching, with very exact rules, all which it is his duty to know that depends on mathematics; as, for instance, the knowledge of encampment, drawing up battalions, fortifications, assaults, planning, surveying, the knowledge of artillery, the use of various instruments, etc.

With all this work in mind, he resigned the professorship at Padua, and moved to Florence. There the Grand Duke Cosmo II gave him a yearly salary that was twice as large as the one he had received at Padua and the title of Philosopher to His Highness. Galileo's first thought was for his family. He asked an advance of two years' salary, and paid the dowry debts to his sisters' husbands.

In 1611, his expenses paid by the Grand Duke, Galileo went to Rome to show his "celestial novelties," as they were called, to the Pope and the cardinals. He was received with great attention, and everyone was delighted to look upon the wonders of the heavens, provided always that nothing could be proved against the supposed assertion of the Bible that the earth did not move!

Galileo soon published his *Discourse on Floating Bodies,* which aroused violent opposition; *Spots Observed on the Body of the Sun,* and the *Discourse on the Tides.* Four years later, he was again in Rome to plead for the Copernican system, and to defend his own conduct in advocating ideas opposed by the Catholic Church. He said:

> I am inclined to think that the authority of Holy Scripture is intended to convince men of those truths which are necessary for their salvations, and which, being far above man's understanding, cannot be made credible by any learning, or any other means than revelation by the Holy Spirit. But that the same God who has endowed us with senses, reason, and understanding does not permit us to use them, and desires to acquaint us in any other way with such knowledge as we are in a position to acquire for ourselves by means of those faculties, *that,* it seems to me, I am not bound to believe, especially concerning those sciences about which the Holy Scriptures contain only small fragments and varying conclusions; and this is precisely the case with astronomy, of which there is so little that the planets are not even all enumerated.

However, in spite of Galileo's logic, the Church decreed that all books which stated the Copernican system as true should be prohibited. This was a great disappointment to Galileo, who loved and revered the Roman Catholic faith. He went home to the Villa Segni, at Bellosguardo, near Florence, and for seven years led a studious and secluded life.

His greatest comfort during these years was the devotion of his daughter, Polissena. While in Padua, Galileo had had three children by Marina Gamba, a Venetian woman of inferior station. She afterwards married a man of her own class, and Galileo took his children to his own home. The son, Vincenzo, was educated as a physician, and the two daughters were placed in a convent.

Polissena, who had taken the name of Sister Maria Celeste when she entered the convent, wrote often to her father. In one of her letters she says:

I put by carefully the letters you write me daily, and when not engaged with my duties, I read them over and over again. This is the greatest pleasure I have. . . .

Again she writes:

. . . I send two baked pears for these days of vigil. But as the greatest treat of all, I send you a rose, which ought to please you extremely, seeing what a rarity it is at this season. . . .

Only in one respect does cloister life weigh heavily on me; that is, that it prevents my attending on you personally, which would be my desire, were it permitted. My thoughts are always with you.

At the end of Galileo's seven years of study near Florence, Urban VIII became Pope, and Galileo and other scientists rejoiced, for he had seemed liberal in thought. Long before, he had sent some verses he had written to Galileo, together with a letter saying, "If not worthy of you, they [the verses] will serve at any rate as a proof of my affection, while I purpose to add luster to my poetry by your renowned name. . . . I beg you to receive with favor this insignificant proof of my affection."

At Eastertime, in the year 1624, Galileo, now sixty years old, resolved to go to Rome to welcome the new Pope and try to persuade him to approve the Copernican theory. Frail in health, he was carried most of the way in a litter. During a visit of six weeks, he had six long audiences with Urban VIII; but though Galileo was warmly received, the Pope remained unconvinced. Instead, he tried to prove to Galileo that he was in error.

The Pope was so kind to him that Galileo went back to Florence with the hope that he could bring out his major work, *Dialogue on the Two Great Systems of the World, the Ptolemaic and Copernican,* without opposition from the Church. In this book Galileo gave the results of a half-century's thought.

The book was ready in March, 1630. To be sure that the Pope did not object to its publication, Galileo decided to go to Rome and personally ask Urban's permission. The Pope gave his consent, provided that the title show that the Copernican system was treated as a hypothesis only, and that he, the Pope, write the closing argument.

Rather than forego the publication of his book, Galileo consented, and returned to Florence. A license to publish was obtained from the Inquisitor-General and the Vicar-General of Florence after great delay. A second and third time the papal authorities wished to look over the manuscript. Two years went slowly by.

Besides the long delay, other anxieties plagued the sixty-eight-year-old Galileo. His brother, Michelangelo, sent his wife, seven children, and a German nurse home to be taken care of. The oldest boy, who had been sent to Rome to study music, turned out to be obstinate, impudent, and dissolute. His father, the shiftless Michelangelo, would not take any responsibility for these "wicked ways" which the boy, he said, "did not learn from me, or anyone else belonging to him. It must have been the fault of his wet nurse!"

Galileo's son, Vincenzo, had also married and brought his wife home to live. The one bright spot in Galileo's life was the daily letter he received from his daughter, Maria Celeste. "But I do not know how to express myself," she wrote, "except by saying that I love you better than myself. For, after God, I belong to you; and your kindnesses are so numberless that I feel I could put my life in peril, were it to save you from any trouble, excepting only that I would not offend His Divine Majesty."

Finally Galileo moved to Arcetri, close to the convent, in order to be near Maria Celeste.

In January, 1632, the *Dialogue* appeared. Copies were sent to his friends and disciples throughout Italy.

The whole country applauded, and at last Galileo seemed to have won the homage he had so long deserved.

But a storm was gathering. Enemies were at work prejudicing the mind of Urban VIII, making him feel that Galileo's book was damaging to the Church. Before long an order came from the Inquisition to secure every copy in the booksellers' shops throughout Italy, and to forward all copies to Rome.

In October of the same year of publication, Galileo was summoned to appear at Rome, to answer to that terror of past centuries, the charge of heresy. His friends pleaded that he was old and feeble, that he would die on the journey; but Urban's commands were absolute.

Galileo was bitter. He wrote a friend:

This vexes me so much that it makes me curse the time devoted to these studies, in which I strove and hoped to deviate somewhat from the beaten track generally pursued by learned men. I not only repent having given the world a portion of my writings, but feel inclined to suppress those still in hand, and to give them to the flames, and thus satisfy the longing desire of my enemies, to whom my ideas are so inconvenient.

On January 20, 1633, the decrepit old man again set out in a litter for Rome, arriving on February 13. Two months later he was brought before the Inquisition. He was examined briefly and then sent back to prison. Although he was treated with leniency, incarceration and worry made him ill and he was confined to his bed until his second appearance before the Inquisition.

Weak, aged, and in fear of torture, Galileo then made the melancholy confession that his "error had been one of vainglorious ambition, and pure ignorance and inadvertence." On May 10, he was summoned a third time before the Inquisition, and told that he had eight days in which to write his defense. In his defense Galileo stated that his book had been examined and re-examined by the authorities, so there might be nothing unorthodox in it; and then he urged the Inquisition to consider his age and feeble health.

On June 22, in the forenoon, in the large hall of the Dominican Convent of St. Maria sopra la Minerva, in the presence of cardinals and prelates, Galileo heard his sentence.

The proposition that the sun is the center of the world and does not move from its place is absurd, and false philosophically, and formally heretical, because it is expressly contrary to the Holy Scripture.

The proposition that the earth is not the center of the world and immovable, but that it moves, and also with a diurnal motion, is equally absurd and false philosophically; and theologically considered, at least erroneous in faith. . . . Invoking, therefore, the most holy name of our Lord Jesus Christ and of His most glorious mother and ever Virgin Mary . . . we say, pronounce, sentence, declare, that you, the said Galileo, by reason of the matters adduced in process, and by you confessed as above, have rendered your-

self, in the judgment of this Holy Office, vehemently suspected of heresy—namely, of having believed and held the
doctrine, which is false and contrary to the sacred and divine
Scriptures—that the sun is the center of the world and does
not move from east to west, and that the earth moves and
is not the center of the world. . . . We condemn you to
the formal prison of this Holy Office during our pleasure,
and, by way of salutary penance, we enjoin that for three
years to come you repeat once a week the seven Penitential
Psalms.

And then the white-haired man of science, kneel-
ing before the whole assembly, made the pitiful abjura-
tion of his belief.

I, Galileo Galilei, son of the late Vincenzo Galilei of
Florence, aged seventy years, being brought personally to
judgment . . . swear that I have always believed, and, with
the help of God, will in future believe, every article which
the Holy Catholic and Apostolic Church of Rome holds,
teaches, and preaches. . . . With a sincere heart and un-
feigned faith, I abjure, curse, and detest the said errors and
heresies, and generally every other error and sect contrary
to the said Holy Church; and I swear that I will never more
in future say, or assert anything, verbally or in writing,
which may give rise to a similar suspicion of me; but that
if I shall know any heretic, or anyone suspected of heresy,
I will denounce him to this Holy Office. . . .

It has been said that Galileo exclaimed as he rose
to his feet, *"E pur si muove,"* "It moves, for all that,"
but this would have been practically impossible, surrounded as he was by men who would instantly have

taken him to a dungeon, and the story is no longer believed.

On July 9, Galileo was allowed to leave Rome for
Siena, where he stayed five months in the house of the
archbishop, and then became a prisoner in his own
house at Arcetri, with strict injunctions that he was
"not to entertain friends, nor allow the assemblage of
many at a time."

He wrote sadly to Maria Celeste, "My name is
erased from the book of the living." Maria Celeste answered that it seemed "a thousand years" since she had
seen him, and that she would recite the seven Penitential Psalms for him, "to save you the trouble of remembering it."

Less than a year later, Maria Celeste died at the
age of thirty-three. Galileo was heartbroken. She was,
he said, "a woman of exquisite mind, singular good-
ness, and most tenderly attached to me."

In the summer of 1636, Galileo completed his
Dialogues on Motion, and sent it to Leyden for publication. The next year he made his last discovery: he
observed the moon's librations, that is, its apparent
rocking motions which enable us to see from earth a
little more than the area of the half sphere.

The house at Arcetri had become dark and lonely.
The wife of Michelangelo, her three daughters, and a
son had all died of the plague. It was doubly dark, for
Galileo had become hopelessly blind, "so that this

heaven, this earth, this universe, which I by my marvelous discoveries and clear demonstrations had enlarged a hundred thousand times beyond the belief of the wise men of bygone ages, henceforward for me is shrunk into such a small space as is filled by my own bodily sensations."

He said later:

I am obliged now to have recourse to other hands and other pens than mine since my sad loss of sight. This, of course, occasions great loss of time, particularly now that my memory is impaired by advanced age; so that in placing my thoughts on paper, many and many a time I am forced to have the foregoing sentences read to me before I can tell what ought to follow; else I should repeat the same thing over and over.

Arrangements for the publication of Galileo's last major work, *The New Sciences*, had to be made in secret. He had planned other work, but death came on the evening of January 8, 1642. His pupils, Torricelli and Viviani, and his son Vincenzo, stood at his bedside.

Galileo had asked to be buried in the family vault of the Galilei in Santa Croce, at Florence, and the city at once voted a public funeral and three thousand crowns for a marble mausoleum. But the Church at Rome forbade it, fearing that it would serve to confirm Galileo's doctrine that the earth moves. Galileo was therefore buried in an obscure corner of Del Noviciato, a side chapel of Santa Croce.

A century later, on March 12, 1737, the bones of Galileo were removed with great ceremony to a new resting place in Santa Croce, where he was buried with his friend, Viviani. An imposing monument was erected over him. As final vindication of his beliefs, the works of Galileo, in sixteen volumes, are no longer prohibited by the Church, as they were in his lifetime.

CHAPTER 3

Isaac Newton

Isaac Newton, only child of Isaac Newton and Hannah Ayscough, was born on Christmas Day, 1642, the same year Galileo died. A few months after his marriage, at the age of thirty-seven, Isaac's father died. Before Isaac was two years old, his mother married again, according to one account: "Mr. Smith, a neighboring clergyman, who had a very good estate, had lived a bachelor till he was pretty old, and, one of his parishioners advising him to marry, he said he did not know where to meet a good wife. The man answered, 'The widow Newton is an extraordinary good woman.' 'But,' said Mr. Smith, 'how do I know she will have me, and I don't care to ask and be denied, but if you will go and ask her, I will pay you for your day's work.'

"He went accordingly. Her answer was, she would

be advised by her brother Ayscough, upon which Mr. Smith sent the same person to Mr. Ayscough on the same errand, who, upon consulting with his sister, treated with Mr. Smith, who gave her son Isaac a parcel of land, one of the terms insisted upon by the widow if she married him."

Mrs. Newton accepted the Reverend Mr. Smith's proposal and went to live at his home, leaving her baby, Isaac, to be reared by his elderly grandmother in a lonely farmhouse in Woolsthorpe, England.

Isaac was so frail that it seemed unlikely that he would live to manhood—or even boyhood. He had been born prematurely and during the first months of his life had to wear a bolster to support his neck. Isaac's childhood was lonely. Until he went to school, he had almost no children to play with; at school he preferred to play alone.

At Grantham, where Isaac went to the public school, he showed little inclination to study. But one day something happened. On his way to school, he got into a fight with a boy who ranked above him in class. Isaac won the fight, and he swore that he would defeat the same boy in scholarship as well. He kept his word, and soon rose to the highest place in the school.

During his school years, Isaac neglected farm chores, preferring to read and make tools and models. He built a small windmill and set it up on top of his house. When there was no wind he used mousepower (a mouse that walked on a treadwheel toward some corn just beyond its reach) to turn the windmill. He also made a large water clock with a circular dial, such as those used today. He invented a four-wheeled carriage that was moved with a handle by the person who sat in it. And he made paper kites, and lanterns of "crimpled paper" with candles inside to light the way to school on the dark winter mornings. Often at night, he would tie a lantern to the tail of one of his kites; sometimes people would mistake these for comets.

On the walls of the farmhouse at Woolsthorpe, Isaac carved sundials, which still could be seen a hundred years later. He was a "sober, silent, thinking lad," who was always hammering in his room, drawing birds and animals, designing ships, and making diagrams with charcoal on the wall.

When he was fifteen, his mother, who had gone back to live with her son a year before, after her second husband died, decided that Isaac should become a farmer. On Saturdays, she would send him with a servant to the market at Grantham to sell grain and other farm produce. But Isaac did not care for the job. Leaving the servant to sell the vegetables, he would hurry to an attic in the house of Mr. Clark, an apothecary with whom he had boarded while at school. There he would spend hours reading old books until the servant had sold the vegetables and it was time to go home. Occasionally Isaac would not get even as far as Grantham, but would settle down by a hedge along the road and read until the servant returned.

When Isaac was sixteen, he experimented with objects of different shapes to see which would offer least resistance when moving in a fluid. He also experimented with wind forces. To test the force of a gale, he jumped first in the direction in which the wind was blowing, and then in the opposite direction. After measuring the length of his leap in both directions and comparing them with the length he could jump on a perfectly calm day, he could compute the force of the gale.

His mother soon found that Isaac would not make a successful farmer, so she sent him back to school at Grantham to prepare for Trinity College, Cambridge, which he entered when he was eighteen.

On July 8, 1661, Newton entered college, where he studied, among other things, Descartes' geometry. Soon he showed marked skill in higher mathematics. By the time he was twenty-two he was studying comets and the circles and halo around the moon.

During the following year, Newton's college was closed because there was a plague in Cambridge, and he returned home to Woolsthorpe. There he remained for eighteen months and during this time made most of the discoveries for which he is famous. Writing in the magazine *Scientific American*, I. Bernard Cohen has called this period of Newton's life "the most fruitful eighteen months in all the history of the creative imagination." During this time, Newton discovered the binomial theorem, the direct method of fluxions (the elements of differential calculus), the inverse method of fluxions (integral calculus), and his theory of gravity.

While sitting alone in his garden at Woolsthorpe, he saw an apple fall to the ground. It occurred to him that the force exerted by the earth on the apple was not measurably less at the tops of buildings or on the peaks of mountains. The earth's attractive force, he decided, might very well extend to the moon, about which he had been studying, and even retain the moon in its orbit. And if to the moon, why not to the planets?

It was also during this period that Newton bought a prism, in order to make some experiments based on Descartes' theory of colors. In a darkened room he made a hole in his window shutter to admit a ray of sunlight, and then he intercepted the ray with his prism. On the opposite wall he saw the solar or prismatic spectrum, an elongated image of the sun, about five times as long as it was broad, and made up of seven different colors: red, orange, yellow, green, blue, indigo, and violet. White light was thus discovered to be a mixture of all the colors. Newton said, "Whiteness is the usual color of light; for light is a confused aggregate of rays endued with all sorts of colors, as they are promiscuously darted from the various parts of luminous bodies." If any one color predominates, the light will incline to that color. For example, a candle flame appears yellow, though it is made up of many different colors.

Before Newton's discovery, there had been all sorts

of conjectures about the nature and origin of colors. Descartes, for instance, regarded color as analogous to musical tones. But Newton showed by many experiments that color is a property of light. We speak of a thing as red because it reflects red, and absorbs all the other colors. A green leaf stops or absorbs the red, blue, and violet rays of white light, and reflects and transmits the green.

Newton also found that the red rays are refracted, or turned out of their course, least of all the colors, and violet most, thereby discovering the different refrangibility of light rays—a discovery that led to the science of spectroscopy and, what is very rare in scientific history, a discovery to which no other person has made the slightest claim.

In 1668, Newton constructed a small reflecting telescope, and soon afterwards, a larger one, which he sent to the Royal Society. He became a fellow of this august honorary association when he was only thirty. Two years before he had been appointed to a professorship of mathematics at Cambridge.

Newton was now spoken of as a man of "unparalleled genius." He had discovered the compound nature of white light, the attraction of gravity, fluxions, and had made the first reflecting telescope ever used in astronomy, although one had been invented previously by James Gregory, of Aberdeen.

Newton's color theory was bitterly opposed—by the great investigator of light, Christian Huygens, among others. In letter after letter to those who wrote to him criticizing it, Newton defended his theory of color. He grew tired of the controversy, became caustic, and threatened never to publish his work again. To Leibnitz, the philosopher and mathematician, he wrote, "I was so persecuted with discussions arising out of my theory of light, that I blamed my own imprudence for parting with so substantial a blessing as my quiet to run after a shadow." To another he wrote, "I see I have made myself a slave to philosophy" (by which he meant physics) ". . . a man must either resolve to put out nothing new, or to become a slave to defend it."

Newton had money difficulties at this time. He asked to be excused from the weekly payments to the Royal Society, thereby resigning his membership, and even thought of studying law as a way to increase his income.

But in spite of his poverty and the opposition to his discoveries, Newton continued his scientific career. When he grew tired of what he was doing, he said he "refreshed himself with history and chronology." Years afterward he published a book, *Chronology of Ancient Kingdoms*.

A man who observed Newton for years while the great scientist was teaching at Cambridge said that he never saw Newton laugh but once. He was, "meek, sedate, and humble, never seemingly angry. I never knew him to take any recreation or pastime, either in riding out to take the air, walking, bowling, or any other exercise whatever, thinking all hours lost that were not spent in his studies, to which he kept so close that he seldom left his chamber except at term time." When Newton lectured, "so few went to hear him, and fewer that understood him, that oftentimes he did in a manner, for want of hearers, read to the walls."

The same observer described Newton's erratic eating and sleeping habits and his absent-mindedness. "So intent, so serious upon his studies that he ate very sparingly, nay, ofttimes he has forgot to eat at all, so that, going to his chamber, I have found his mess untouched, of which when I have reminded him he would reply, 'Have I?' and then making to the table, would eat a bit or two standing, for I cannot say I ever saw him sit at a table by himself. . . .

"He very rarely went to bed until two or three of the clock, sometimes not till five or six, lying about four or five hours, especially at spring and fall of the leaf, at which times he used to employ about six weeks in his laboratory, the fire scarcely going out either night or day. . . ."

When his most intense studies were carried on, "he learned to go to bed at twelve, finding by experience that if he exceeded that hour but a little, it did him more harm in his health than a whole day's study.

"He rarely went to dine in the hall, except on some public days, and then if he has not been minded, would go very carelessly, with shoes down at heels, stockings untied, surplice on, and his head scarcely combed. . . . At some seldom times when he designed to dine in the hall, he would turn to the left hand and go out into the street, when making a stop when he found his mistake, would hastily turn back, and then sometimes, instead of going into the hall, would return to his chamber again. . . ."

Isaac Newton was definitely absent-minded. Once, so a story goes, on his way home to Colsterworth, he led his horse up a hill. When he decided to remount, he discovered that the horse had slipped the bridle and run away. Newton had held the bridle in his hand for some time without noticing that there was no horse in it.

In 1687, when Newton was forty-five, his *Philosophia Naturalis Principia Mathematica* was published. The *Principia,* as it is always called, consists of three "books." In the first Newton deals with laws of force and their consequences. Here his three well-known laws of motion appear. The second book concerns the oscillations of pendulums and motion in different fluids. Newton demonstrates in his third book how the same force explains the falling of bodies on earth, the motion of the moon and of planets, and the phenomenon of tides. And he states his great principle of universal gravitation: that every body in the universe attracts every other body with a force that is directly proportional to the product of their masses and inversely proportional to the square of the distance between them.

By the laws of gravity, Newton was able to calculate the quantity of matter in the sun, and in all the planets, and even to determine their density, results which the economist Adam Smith said later, "were above the reach of human reason and experience." He ascertained that the weight of the same body would be twenty-three times greater at the surface of the sun than at the surface of the earth, and that the density of the earth was four times greater than that of the sun.

The *Principia* has been called "a work which will be memorable not only to the annals of one science or of one country, but which will form an epoch in the history of the world, a work which would be read with delight in every planet of our system, in every system of the universe. What a glorious privilege was it to have been the author of the *Principia!*"

Publication of the *Principia* created excitement, speculation, and violent opposition throughout Europe. Some scientists acclaimed it, but the majority could not believe that an invisible force exerted by the sun kept the planets in their orbits.

When Newton presented copies of his book to the heads of colleges, some of them said "they might study seven years before they understood anything of it."

Newton also published his work on the calculus (fluxions) at this time, because Leibnitz's book, *Differ-*

ential Calculus, had just come out and it contained much of the same material. Newton and Leibnitz both claimed priority in the discovery of the calculus, and they and their followers argued hotly about it. Today historians of science agree that the two men had made the same discovery independently.

After this episode, Newton, fearful and suspicious of other scientists, guarded his work jealously. His letters reveal that for a time he was nervous and emotionally upset. He had trouble sleeping and accused his friends of treating him badly—accusations for which he later apologized.

In 1689, when he was forty-seven, Newton was chosen Member of Parliament, and represented Cambridge University in the House of Commons for thirteen months. Other official positions were sought for him from time to time by his friends—among them John Locke—for his labors had brought him very little income. Finally, when he was fifty-three, the influence of his friend Charles Montague, Earl of Halifax, helped him out of his difficulties. Lord Halifax appointed him Warden of the Mint, and then Master, with an income of between six thousand and seventy-five hundred dollars annually. He held this position for the rest of his life. In his home in London, where he kept six servants, he had a companion—Catherine Barton, his niece. Lord Halifax was a great admirer of Catherine Barton. At his death, he left her a home and twenty-five thousand dollars "as a small recompense for the pleasure and happiness I have had in her conversation."

Newton's days of privation were over. Great people often came to dine with him. At one of his dinners, he proposed to drink, not to the health of kings and princes, but to all honest persons, to whatever country they belonged. "We are all friends," he added, "because we unanimously aim at the only object worthy of man, which is the knowledge of truth. We are also of the same religion, because, leading a simple life we conform ourselves to what is right, and we endeavor sincerely to give to the Supreme Being that worship which, according to our feeble lights, we are persuaded will please him most."

In 1703, Newton was elected President of the Royal Society, and was annually re-elected during the remaining twenty-five years of his life. When he was sixty-three, he was knighted by Queen Anne. The previous year his great work on optics, written over twenty years before, had been published.

About this time, Sir Isaac would have liked to marry Lady Norris, the widow of a baronet. Sir William Norris had been Lady Norris' third husband, and Sir Isaac, now over sixty, wanted to be the fourth. He wrote her this letter:

Madam,—Your ladyship's great grief at the loss of Sir William shows that if he had returned safe home, your ladyship could have been glad to have lived still with a husband,

and therefore your aversion at present from marrying again can proceed from nothing else than the memory of him whom you have lost. To be always thinking on the dead, is to live a melancholy life among sepulchres, and how much grief is an enemy to your health, is very manifest by the sickness it brought when you received the first news of your widowhood. And can your ladyship resolve to spend the rest of your days in grief and sickness?

Can you resolve to wear a widow's habit perpetually —a habit which is less acceptable to company, a habit which will be always putting you in mind of your lost husband, and thereby promote your grief and indisposition till you leave it off? The proper remedy for all these mischiefs is a new husband, and whether your ladyship should admit of a proper remedy for such maladies, is a question which I hope will not need much time to consider of.

Whether your ladyship should go constantly in the melancholy dress of a widow, or flourish once more among the ladies; whether you should spend the rest of your days cheerfully or in sadness, in health or in sickness, are questions which need not much consideration to decide them. Besides that, your ladyship will be better able to live according to your quality by the assistance of a husband than upon your own estate alone; and therefore, since your ladyship likes the person proposed, I doubt not but in a little time to have notice of your ladyship's inclinations to marry, at least, that you will give him leave to discourse with you about it.

I am, madam, your ladyship's most humble and most obedient servant.

While Lady Norris may have "liked the person proposed," she and Newton never married.

In his last years Newton, whose religious views were not at all orthodox, wrote about mysticism, alchemy, and the occult. When he was eighty-three he published a third edition of the *Principia*. At eighty-five he could read without glasses, and his mind was as accurate as ever, although his memory was failing.

On March 2, 1727, he presided at a meeting of the Royal Society. He was taken ill on the following day, and died on March 20.

Isaac Newton was buried in Westminster Abbey. A statue of him was erected at Trinity College, where he had done so much of his work when little more than a boy.

A short time before his death Newton spoke of his achievements: "I do not know what I may appear to the world, but to myself I seem to have been only like a boy playing on the seashore, and diverting myself in now and then finding a smoother pebble or a prettier shell than ordinary, whilst the great ocean of truth lay all undiscovered before me."

CHAPTER 4

William Herschel

William Herschel was born in Hanover, Germany, on November 15, 1738, one of four boys in a family of ten children. His father, Isaac Herschel, was a musician who played the oboe in the royal band. When, during the Seven Years' War, his health failed, he made a living by giving music lessons in his home.

There was a military fort in Hanover, and the Herschel children went to a school there, studying French and English as well as the usual subjects. After school, their father taught them music. William learned French and English rapidly and also studied Latin and arithmetic. He was so passionately fond of reading that his mother was alarmed. She could not even write and she distrusted signs of intellectual development in her children.

Mrs. Herschel was able to prevent her daughters from learning French or drawing, but she was less successful with William. Caroline, the eighth child, who was twelve years younger than William, looked upon her brother as a genius.

William and his younger brother, Alexander, played in the orchestra of the court, and sometimes gave solo performances, Alexander on the violincello, William playing the harpsichord. After a concert, the brothers would come home and talk about music or science until late at night—sometimes even until dawn —and their father would join in with enthusiasm. They sounded so excited and happy during these midnight talks that Caroline would try to stay awake to hear what they were saying. When they talked about science, they would often argue quite hotly, and she would hear shouted the names of the great scientists Newton, Leibnitz, and Euler. Then Mrs. Herschel would interrupt the arguers, saying that their loud voices would disturb the younger children, who had to be in school by seven in the morning.

William and Alexander would go to their room, where they shared the same bed, and continue talking —at least William would, for he "had still a great deal to say; and frequently it happened that when he stopped for an assent or reply, he found his hearer was gone to sleep, and I suppose," Caroline adds, "it was not till then that he bethought himself to do the same."

Mr. Herschel was interested in astronomy. Once

he took Caroline out at night to see a comet that was visible at the time and then lingered to point out the constellations to her. He liked to help William with projects and experiments. Together they made a small globe on which William engraved the ecliptic and the equator.

William's interest in science was so great that, in his sister's opinion, he might have made important discoveries while he was young. But time for his own studies was something William didn't have. His family had little money and he had to find a way to support himself.

For a time he served in the Hanover foot guards. When he was seventeen, the guards were sent to England for a year, and he went with them. There he discovered John Locke's influential book, *Essay Concerning Human Understanding,* which argues that reason, rather than faith, "must be our last guide and judge in everything."

When William returned to Hanover, he brought a copy of Locke's book with him. He soon left the foot guards, because his health was not very good, and decided to return to England and try to earn a living there.

William was nineteen years old when he left for England the second time. For the next three years, little is known about him, except that he sometimes played at concerts and with military bands. There was little indication then that he would someday become a great astronomer.

When William Herschel was twenty-four, he found a permanent job as organist at the Octagon Chapel, in Bath, a well-known English winter resort. He supplemented his income by giving music lessons, and although he spent fourteen or sixteen hours a day with his students, found time to compose music for the cathedral choir. In whatever spare moments he had, he studied Greek and Italian. Before going to sleep at night, he would relax by reading books on calculus, optics, and astronomy.

In 1767, William's father died. Caroline went to work as a seamstress, and William wanted her to come to live with him in England. He wrote to her, offering to give her singing lessons. If her voice developed well, she could sing with the choir.

But Caroline did not come to England and finally, in 1772, William went back to Germany to fetch her. She returned to Bath with him, began her singing lessons, and also studied arithmetic and accounting so that she could run William's house efficiently. Alexander, who had come to England earlier, was also living in William's house; now Caroline and Alexander shared the attic.

It soon became apparent to Caroline that, instead of being trained to sing, she was being trained as handyman to an astronomer. Day after day, she waited in vain for her singing lesson; but William was busy, teaching himself astronomy. During the spring, when the resort people no longer came to Bath and William had fewer music students, Caroline thought her brother would have more time for her. But this was not the case. William, exhausted after a winter of hard work, spent much of his time in bed with astronomy books and "went to sleep buried under his favorite authors; and his first thoughts on rising were how to obtain the instruments for viewing these objects himself of which he had been reading."

Herschel could not afford to buy a telescope, but he found one—two and one-half feet long—that he could rent. He spent his time observing the stars with it or taking it apart to find out how it was made. Soon he was trying to build a telescope of his own and called Caroline away from her musical practice, "my help being continually wanted in the execution of the various contrivances." She helped him make a pasteboard tube "eighteen or twenty feet long" into which the lenses of the telescope, which had to be ordered from London, were fitted. It was a failure; the pasteboard tube was too flexible to remain straight.

Herschel solved the problem by substituting tin tubes. Soon the whole house was turned into a workshop. In the handsomely furnished drawing room a cabinetmaker worked on tubes and stands. In a bedroom, Alexander operated a large machine for grinding lenses and turning eyepieces and other telescope parts.

Herschel had one unalterable purpose in his life —the study of astronomy. Nothing ever drew him from it. Too poor to buy telescopes, he made them. With no time to read books during the day, he took the hours from sleep. With little opportunity for education, he educated himself.

By 1774 Herschel had acquired considerable mechanical skill and knowledge of telescopes. He made a 5½-foot Gregorian telescope (the eye of the observer is in line with the telescope and the stars in this model); a year later he built a Newtonian telescope (using this, the observer's eye is at right angles to the line formed between telescope and stars). The latter instrument had a 4½-inch aperture and magnified 222 times.

Now Herschel was equipped for serious astronomical study, but he had little time to spend on it. He was still forced to give music lessons to support himself and, in addition, he had become director of a one-hundred-piece orchestra that played in a theater. As soon as an act was over, so the story goes, he would rise from his seat before the harpsichord and rush out of the theater to look at the stars.

At this time Herschel was making a seven-foot reflector; then he made a ten-foot reflector. These were fashioned by hand since machines for the purpose were not invented until about ten years later. His brother

Alexander continued to assist him and Caroline's time "was taken up with copying music and practicing, besides attendance on my brother when polishing; since, by way of keeping him alive, I was constantly obliged to feed him, by putting his victuals by bits into his mouth. This was once the case, when, in order to finish a seven-foot mirror, he had not taken his hands from it for sixteen hours together. In general he was never unemployed at meals, but was always at those times contriving or making drawings of whatever came in his mind. Generally I was obliged to read to him while he was at the turning-lathe, or polishing mirrors, *Don Quixote, Arabian Nights' Entertainment,* the novels of Sterne, Fielding, etc.; serving tea and supper without interrupting the work with which he was engaged."

Herschel, who was now forty years old, began to study every visible star of the first, second, third, and fourth magnitude. He observed the moon and measured the height of its mountains.

His work began to receive attention. Two of his papers, one on the periodical star in Collo Ceti, the other on the mountains of the moon, were read at a meeting of the Royal Society, and Herschel also became a member of the Philosophical Society of Bath.

In a paper written when he was forty-three, Herschel says: "I began to construct a thirty-foot aerial reflector, and having made a stand for it, I cast the mirror thirty-six inches in diameter. This was cracked in cooling. I cast it a second time, and the furnace I had built in my house broke." On the night of Tuesday, March 13, he wrote: "In examining the small stars in the neighborhood of *H. Geminorum* I perceived one that appeared visibly larger than the rest; being struck with its uncommon appearance, I compared it to *H. Geminorum* and the small star in the quarter between Auriga and Gemini, and finding it so much larger than either of them, I suspected it to be a comet." The orbit of this "comet" was computed and its distance from the sun found to be 1,800 million miles.

The world soon was notified that a new planet had been found—the greatest astronomical discovery since Galileo had trained his telescope on the skies. Herschel became famous overnight. (So little was he known previously that one journal called him "Mersthel," another "Herthel," and still another "Hermstel.") In December of the same year, 1781, he was elected a Fellow of the Royal Society, England's most distinguished scientific group, and received the Copley Gold Medal. He called the new planet Georgium Sidus, in honor of George III, who was then king of England, but the name was later changed to Uranus, after Urania, the muse of astronomy. Some years later Herschel discovered two of Uranus' satellites, Titania and Oberon.

Eagerly, Herschel went on with his work. He erected a stand for his twenty-foot telescope in the garden and perfected the mirror, which had to be cast in a furnace. Whenever he could find a moment between music lessons or by giving one of his students the slip, he would check "to see how the men went on with the furnace, which was built in a room below, even with the garden. . . . The mirror for the thirty-foot reflector was never out of his mind."

The next year, 1782, Herschel visited London, where he was received by George III. He wrote to his sister from London, telling her of his success:

Dear Lina,

All my papers are printing, with the postscripts and all, and are allowed to be very valuable. You see, Lina, I tell you all these things. You know vanity is not my foible, therefore I need not fear your censure. Farewell.

I am your affectionate brother,

Wm. Herschel

Again he wrote:

I pass my time between Greenwich and London, agreeably enough, but am rather at a loss for work that I like. Company is not always pleasing, and I would much rather be polishing a speculum. . . . I am introduced to the best company. Tomorrow I dine at Palmerston's, next day with Sir Joseph Banks, etc., etc. Among opticians and astronomers nothing now is talked of but what they call my great discoveries. Alas! this shows how far they are behind, when such trifles as I have seen and done are called great. Let me but get at it again! I will make such telescopes, and see such things—that is, I will endeavor to do so.

George III appointed Herschel Royal Astronomer, with an annual salary of one thousand dollars. Now Herschel would not have to depend on his musical ability to earn a living and could spend all his time on astronomy. He went back to Bath to say goodbye to his pupils and to play for the last time in the chapel. Then he moved to the town of Datchet, set up his telescope, and began to make systematic surveys, or sweeps, of the sky.

He would count every visible star in a given field, surveying 683 fields in all. From the observations he made, he deducted that our galaxy was shaped like a flattened grindstone. This was the first study of its kind and though many have been done since, with telescopes far more powerful than Herschel's, the shape he discovered for our galaxy still substantially holds true.

Herschel worked outside in the garden and the temperature there was often as low as thirteen degrees. This did not deter him. If the weather was clear, he would stand at his telescope the whole night through, regardless of the temperature, only going indoors for a few minutes every three or four hours. He followed this routine for many years, always working outside, because his telescope only performed well when it was the same temperature as the air.

Herschel began his astronomical surveys as soon as he moved to Datchet, without waiting for his telescope to be firmly installed. Caroline watched him as he worked fifteen feet above the ground, standing on a temporary crossbeam which was supported by ladders that "had not even their braces at the bottom. One night, in a very high wind, he had hardly touched ground before the whole apparatus came down." Caroline adds that she "could give a pretty long list of accidents which were near proving fatal to my brother as well as myself."

Another person who watched Herschel at his telescope in the icy garden commented, "He has an excellent constitution and thinks about nothing else in the world but the celestial bodies."

Although Herschel was occupied with celestial bodies, he still found time to think about other things. On May 8, 1783, when he was forty-five, he married the wealthy widow of John Pitt. When William's new wife moved into his home, Caroline moved out of it. For more than twenty years she lived apart from the brother she loved so well, but paid him a visit every day to help him with his work. Sometimes, when Mrs. Herschel was away, Caroline would stay with William for a few days, but she always went back to her lodgings when Mrs. Herschel returned. As time passed, however, she became more reconciled to William's wife and, in a letter, called her "a dear sister, for as such I now know you." Nine years after their marriage, a son was born to the Herschels. They named him John and he grew up to become an important astronomer. Caroline idolized him.

In 1785 Herschel began to build his great forty-foot telescope. George III had given him twenty thousand dollars for this project, as well as a thousand dollars a year for the telescope's maintenance. It took two years to build the instrument, which was so large that a man could walk through it. During this time the Herschels moved to the town of Slough, near Windsor, and the unfinished telescope was moved with them. Then the construction continued. Herschel has described it:

In the whole of the apparatus none but common workmen were employed, for I made drawings of every part of it, by which it was easy to execute the work, as I constantly inspected and directed every person's labor; though sometimes there were not less than forty different workmen employed at the same time. While the stand of the telescope was preparing, I also began the construction of the great mirror, of which I inspected the casting, grinding, and polishing. . . .

He made improvements in telescope design—the Herschelian model has a single speculum, or reflector—and supervised the manufacture of hundreds of reflectors that were sent all over the world. When his own great telescope was completed, his work went forward rapidly. He discovered two satellites of Saturn, Mimas and Enceladus; and showed that another of Saturn's satellites, Japetus, turns once on its axis in each revolution about Saturn, just as the moon does about the earth.

He studied the sun, its probably gaseous surface and its spots, and was the first to suspect their periodic character. (He did not know that the sunspots are as much as one billion square miles in size, more than five times the surface of the earth.) He saw, as astronomers today see, that heat cannot be produced without expenditure of energy; and that the sun is probably cooling, although this will scarcely be perceptible on earth for ages to come. He understood the rise and fall of the solar system: how gradually, through almost countless centuries, it became fit for life, for the coming of man; how finally it would become unfit and man would vanish from the earth.

Herschel studied the Milky Way. At first he thought that it was entirely composed of stars, about eighteen million of them; but later he changed his theory, when he found that the Milky Way contained much nebulous matter—matter in a state of condensation, as if new worlds were forming, possibly to become the homes of a new race or of future generations of man. In all, he discovered twenty-five hundred new nebulae and clusters.

Herschel's conclusions about variable stars received much attention at the time they were published, but have not as yet been confirmed. He observed that the star Mira Ceti was invisible to the naked eye for several months, then grew brighter and brighter, and finally disappeared again, completing the cycle. Many other stars, he discovered, are periodic, and he decided that this was caused by the star's rotation on its axis, so that different parts of its surface are presented periodically. Today, however, there is still no satisfactory explanation for long-period variable stars, like Mira.

He made a catalogue of double, or binary, stars and, after laborious calculations, established that such stars have a common center of gravity; that one star revolves about another. He inferred that our solar system is traveling toward a point in the constellation Hercules.

Assessing Herschel's contribution to his science, an astronomer once said:

> It is the groundwork upon which we have still to build. . . . As a scientific conception it is perhaps the grandest that has ever entered into the human mind. As a study of the height to which the efforts of one man may go, it is almost without a parallel. . . . By a kindly chance he can be claimed as the citizen of no one country. In very truth his is one of the few names which belong to the whole world.

Until Herschel was seventy-six, he was active in his work, and Caroline continued to assist him. He made a telescope for her, and with it she spied eight comets, five of which had never been seen before. She also compiled several catalogues of stars and a lengthy reference index. When these were published, Caroline was recognized as a scientist in her own right and became an honorary member of the Royal Astronomical Society.

In his late seventies, Herschel's health began to fail and he frequently took little trips away from Slough for a change of scene and air. Caroline stayed at home to copy his papers for the Royal Society. In 1816 he was made a knight of the Royal Hanoverian Guelphic Order, by the Prince Regent, and five years later he became the first president of the newly formed Royal Astronomical Society.

As Herschel grew older and weaker, Caroline often found him very depressed. One day—he was eighty at the time—he was getting ready for a short trip to Bath with his wife. Probably because he feared he might die leaving his papers in disorder, he asked Caroline to make an inventory of his work. "The last moments before he stepped into the carriage," says Caroline, "were spent in walking with me through his library and workrooms, pointing with anxious looks to every shelf and drawer, desiring me to examine all and to make memorandums of them as well as I could. He was hardly able to support himself, and his spirits were so low, that I found difficulty in commanding my voice. . . ."

On a day in July, when Herschel was eighty-one, he sent a note to his sister:

Lina,—
There is a great comet. I want you to assist me. Come to dine and spend the day here. If you can come soon after one o'clock we shall have time to prepare maps and telescopes. I saw its situation last night—it has a long tail.

Caroline wrote on this small slip of yellow paper: "I keep this as a relic!" A month later William Herschel became very sick. As long as he had any strength, he tried to work and worried about his scientific records. One day, when he could no longer leave his room, Caroline went to see him as usual and, "As soon as he saw me, I was sent to the library to fetch one of his last papers and a plate of the forty-foot telescope. But for the universe I could not have looked twice at what I had snatched from the shelf, and when he faintly asked if the breaking up of the Milky Way was in it, I said 'Yes!' and he looked content. I cannot help remembering this circumstance, it was the last time I was sent to the library on such an occasion."

William Herschel died on August 25, 1822. After he was buried, in the church at Upton, Windsor, Caroline went home to Germany, "a person," she said, "that has nothing more to do in this world." She lived simply in Hanover with her brother, Dietrich, not spending half of the five hundred dollars a year left her by William, and died when she was almost ninety-eight. A lock of her brother's hair was placed in her coffin, as she had requested.

Eighteen years after William Herschel's death, the wooden parts of his great forty-foot telescope rotted, and the instrument was taken down and placed on its side. After commemorative ceremonies, the telescope was sealed and put on piers, as a scientific monument.

Through this telescope, Herschel once said, "I have looked further into space than ever human being did before me. I have observed stars of which the light takes two millions of years to travel to this globe."

CHAPTER 5

Michael Faraday

Few physicists have started out with as little as Michael Faraday, who discovered the induction of electricity. He had no money, almost no formal education, and—most startling of all—little knowledge of mathematics. Yet as well as discovering the principle of the electric generator and producing the first dynamo, this poor, "uneducated" Englishman formulated the idea of "field"—an idea fundamental to James Clerk Maxwell's electromagnetic theory and Einstein's theory of relativity.

Michael Faraday was born on September 22, 1791, ten years after the end of the American Revolution. His father was a blacksmith; his mother was almost illiterate. When Michael was nine years old, his father's health failed and he could not earn enough to feed his family of four. The Faradays managed to get public relief, and Michael's portion was a loaf of bread. He had to make this last for a week.

The Faradays, who were living in London on the top floor of an old coach house, couldn't afford to keep Michael in school. So he learned only, as he put it, "the rudiments of reading, writing, and arithmetic." At thirteen, he found a job. He worked for a bookseller named Riebau, first as an errand boy and then, after a year, as an apprentice in the bookbinding department. There he began to read the books he handled every day and in his diary wrote the titles of some that he liked especially: Marcet's *Conversations in Chemistry,* Watt's *Improvement of the Mind,* and the article on electricity in the *Encyclopaedia Britannica.* He was very imaginative and said later that as a boy it was as easy for him to believe the *Arabian Nights* as an encyclopedia.

Michael made some simple experiments when he was a boy, but he had no money for apparatus or books and there were no night schools he could attend. So although he was avid for more scientific knowledge, he had little chance to obtain it. One day, when he was nineteen, he saw a sign in a shop window announcing a series of lectures on natural science. These cost a shilling each. Fortunately, Michael's brother, who had become a blacksmith, was able to give him a little money.

Michael attended the talks, took extensive notes, and, with the help of an artist he met at the lectures, added illustrations. Then in his spare moments at the bookbindery, he bound his notes. They made four volumes. Now he had some scientific books of his own.

Michael had lost interest in bookbinding long ago. He wanted desperately to become a scientist and had applied to the Royal Society for a job—without success. Finally, he saw an opportunity. One of the customers at the bookshop had invited him to some lectures on chemistry given by a renowned scientist, Sir Humphry Davy. Again Michael took copious notes. He sent these to Sir Humphry with a note asking for help with his career.

A few days later the Davy carriage stopped before Michael's door, and the footman gave him the following note:

Sir:
  I am far from displeased with the proof you have given me of your confidence, and which displays a great zeal, power of memory, and attention. I am obliged to go out of town, and shall not be settled till the end of January. I will then see you at any time you wish. It would gratify me to be of any service to you. I wish it may be in my power.
  I am, sir,
                              Your obedient humble servant,
                              H. Davy

There is reason to think that Davy's action was motivated more by vanity than a sincere interest in Michael. (Later, when Faraday was proposed for membership in the Royal Society, Davy voted against him out of jealousy, according to some historians.) But whatever the reason, Sir Humphry gave Faraday his start in science. He worked for the famous man first as secretary and later as laboratory assistant.

Faraday learned fast, both in the laboratory and away from it. He joined a scientific society and persuaded some of the members to start a study group. They worked independently and once a week met in Faraday's lodgings to talk over their studies.

In these days he was too busy for love. He was fond of telling people that there were no women in his life and that he felt no need for any. He even wrote and published a poem that criticized falling in love. Nevertheless, when he was twenty-nine, he fell very much in love and married the girl, who was named Sarah Barnhard. Their marriage lasted fifty years and reportedly was a very happy one.

When Michael Faraday was twenty-two, Sir Humphry took him on a tour of Europe. This lasted for two years and gave Michael the opportunity to meet many well-known scientists, who later helped him in his work. After this trip, he went back to Davy's laboratory at the Royal Institution, where he worked for the rest of his life. It was here that he discovered benzene, produced the first "stainless steel," and worked out his laws of electrolysis.

Faraday was doing research in chemistry when, in 1820, he heard of the discovery that an electric current could produce magnetism. He began to wonder whether the reverse was also true, whether a magnet could produce electricity. In a series of experiments he tried to produce this effect, but failed. Then he gave up for a while and went back to chemistry research. Finally, in 1831, following his discovery that a magnet would revolve around a current-carrying wire, he performed his most famous experiment. Plunging a bar magnet quickly into a coil of wire, he observed that a current was generated in the coil. He obtained this current whether he moved the magnet or the coil; the crucial point was that the relative motion of the conductor and the magnetic field caused the current. Once he knew this, it wasn't hard to produce a continuous electric current; he had made the first dynamo.

Faraday was not satisfied, however. He wondered what caused the electromagnetic induction that he had discovered. His investigation led him to the idea that all space is filled with various lines of force: electric, magnetic, radiant, thermal, and gravitational. This was the beginning of the concept of field that led directly to the theories of Maxwell and Einstein and to a revolution in physics. Before Michael Faraday, all physical processes were explained fundamentally in terms of the particle. After Faraday, the field, as well as the particle, was regarded as fundamental.

Faraday received many honors for his electromagnetic discoveries, but these were not important to him. He turned down honorary degrees and refused the presidency of the Royal Institution and the Royal Society. He even refused to be knighted. All of his scientific work was what today we would call "basic research." When one of his projects developed to the point where it had commercial possibilities, Faraday would give it up.

His indifference to money and fame and his passionate interest in knowledge for its own sake mystified some people. The influential prime minister, William Gladstone, once watched Faraday at an experiment. The results seemed unimportant to the master politician. "Of what *use* is such a discovery?" he wanted to know.

Faraday sprang back with, "Why, you will soon be able to tax it!" He was often asked questions like Gladstone's and sometimes replied, quoting Benjamin Franklin, "Of what use is a newborn child?"

Although Faraday was indifferent to the things that many people value most highly, he was not indifferent to people. He said once that the "sweetest reward" he had received for his work was the good will shown him by people everywhere. He thought it was very important to explain the work that he and other scientists had done so that it could be understood by all who cared to listen, and he frequently gave lectures. It was said that "his manner was absolutely natural, his sympathy with his audience perfect, and his explanations such that the ignorant could understand enough to be interested and the learned could follow him beyond the bounds of their own knowledge." His lectures were always crowded.

Gradually, during Faraday's lifetime, the public began to recognize his achievements. The government granted him a small sum of money each year and Queen Victoria gave him a house on Hampton Court Green, where he lived until his death, on August 25, 1867. He was buried in Highgate Cemetery with, as he had requested, "only a gravestone of the most ordinary kind" to mark the spot.

CHAPTER 6

Lord Kelvin

Lord Kelvin (William Thomson in private life) is rated as one of the world's great physicists. He taught, and himself acted on the belief, that "the best performance of the everyday occupations of mankind are those to which the principles of science are rigidly applied." The term "applied science" has been given to the kind of work which he thus instituted.

Lord Kelvin's achievements were many and diverse. He formulated the dissipation of energy principle that is summarized in the second law of thermodynamics. His knowledge of engineering made it possible to lay the first telegraph cable across the Atlantic Ocean. He invented a temperature scale, instruments for receiving cable signals, a mariner's compass, and a deep-sea sounding apparatus. He made significant contributions to the theories of elasticity, magnetism, vortex motion, and electricity. His lectures fill three volumes; his articles seven.

William Thomson was born in Belfast, Ireland, on June 26, 1824. He was the second son of Professor James Thomson, head of the mathematical department of the Royal Academical Institution—whose family originally had emigrated from Scotland to escape religious persecution. William's mother, who was the daughter of a Glasgow merchant, died while her children were still young and Professor Thomson alone reared his five sons and three daughters.

In 1832, when William was eight years old, his father went to teach in the mathematical department of Glasgow University, the same university where one day William would also teach. Even before William's time, Thomsons were not unusual among the Glasgow faculty. In fact there were so many of them that students and townsmen often spoke of the school as the Thomsonian University.

Both William and his elder brother, James, showed remarkable mental abilities when they were boys. At the ages of ten and twelve respectively they were able to pass entrance examinations at the university. There they held their own among their fellow students although their subjects were difficult. They studied Newton's *Principia,* Lagrange's mathematical work, *Theory of Functions,* as well as philosophy, logic, chemistry, Latin, and Greek. Competition in their class was keen; one of their fellow-students was John Caird, who afterwards became head of the university.

In the summer of 1840, Professor Thomson took William and James with him on a tour through Germany. He wanted the two boys to have an opportunity to study the German language at first hand. Unfortunately for the success of this project, William discovered a book—Fourier's work on mathematical physics—which completely absorbed him, and had a deep influence on his later career. He had no time for speaking German.

In 1841, on his father's advice, William entered St. Peter's. There he was assigned to a tutor, as the custom was, and began to study mathematics. Before long he was contributing articles to the *Cambridge Mathematical Journal* and gained a reputation for brilliance. He was also interested in rowing and swimming and showed such aptitude for music that he was made president of the university musical society.

The highest honor a student of mathematics could win in those days was top place on the Cambridge Mathematical Tripos lists—in other words, highest score in the tripos contest. Those who competed in the contest were called "Wranglers," and the student who came out ahead was known as "Senior Wrangler." Every mathematics student aspired to this honor, and William, whose record was outstanding so far, had a good chance to win it. He and his father anxiously awaited the results of the examination. The post of professor of natural science was vacant at Glasgow University. Professor Thomson wanted his son to get the post, and it would probably be his if he became Senior Wrangler.

When the results of the tripos contest were announced, William was second on the list. A student named Parkinson, from another college, had won the top honor. However, there was another mathematical award, Smith's Prize, for which William still had a chance. He entered the competition, as did Parkinson; this time William placed first and Parkinson second. After the competition, one of the examiners said to another, "You and I are just about fit to mend young Thomson's pen."

Soon after William won Smith's Prize and acquired a title for himself after all—"Smith's Prizeman"—he was offered the professorship he wanted at Glasgow. But before he settled in Scotland, he went to Paris to study under the great physicist Regnault, who was working in thermodynamics. William also visited London, where he met Michael Faraday.

When he began to teach at Glasgow University, where he remained for fifty-three years, William Thomson was twenty-two years old. His first, or inaugural, lecture was an outline of the scope and methods of physics. It was considered an excellent piece of work but was badly presented because Thomson was so nervous.

As time passed, he lost his self-consciousness and went to the other extreme, often forgetting during a class that he was talking to students and not to himself. Something in the subject matter would suggest an idea to him and he would cover the blackboards with figures that meant nothing to his audience. Many of his pupils were present only because their course required a certain number of credits in physics. They made no effort to follow their professor on these intellectual excursions and consequently were bored. "I listened to his lectures on the pendulum for a month," one of his students said, "and all I know about the thing yet is that it wags."

Professor Thomson was popular, however, with students who loved physics. They were interested in his digressions and appreciated the way he used clear physical meanings instead of stereotyped textbook phrases. They went to him for help with their own scientific projects—both when they were students and later in life—and he gave them complete attention, encouragement, and enlightened criticism.

Sometimes in class Thomson illuminated a point with lightning clearness. For example, he once asked a student to explain the meaning of the symbol dx/dt. "Sir," answered the young man, "it denotes the limiting value of the ratio of the increment of x to the increment of t when the latter increment is indefinitely diminished." "Hmm," observed Thomson shortly, "that's what Todhunter would say. Does nobody know that it represents a velocity?"

Fortunately for Professor Thomson's own research, the university sessions lasted only six months of the year, and he was left with considerable free time for his own work. Some of this had to do with electricity. He discovered how to determine the unit of current in both the volt and the ampere and established the measuring unit known as the standard ohm by applying to his measurements of the volt and ampere the consequences of Ohm's Law.

He played a part, too, in one of the most dramatic discoveries of the twentieth century—wireless telegraphy. That it was possible to produce an oscillatory current in a Leyden jar had first been postulated by Joseph Henry. This idea had been regarded as a rather wild speculation until Thomson, in a brilliant paper delivered before the Glasgow Philosophical Society, confirmed Henry's idea. (Later it was proved experimentally by still another physicist.) In the same paper, Thomson presented a formula for determining the rapidity of the oscillations. Building on these ideas, James Clerk Maxwell, a contemporary of Thomson, showed that if the oscillations could be made sufficiently rapid, much of the energy stored in a Leyden jar could be radiated into space in the form of electromagnetic waves. Heinrich Hertz developed the idea still further. Not only did he produce such waves, he devised a method for receiving them—and then it only remained for such men as Marconi and Sir Oliver Lodge to work out the practical applications and make wireless telegraphy a reality.

Before he settled down at Glasgow University,

Thomson had gone to Paris to study thermodynamics, or the theoretical relationship between work and heat. His teacher, Regnault, had done some important experiments on steam, and the French physicist, Nicolas Carnot, had discovered that it was possible to convert mechanical work into heat and that the reverse was also true: heat could be converted into work. Moreover, he had found that to a given amount of mechanical work there is a corresponding definite amount of heat. Little attention had been paid to these discoveries, but Thomson thought they were important. He wrote an article about them that was widely discussed by other scientists and gave these discoveries the attention they deserved.

Thomson himself did research in the field of thermodynamics, research that led to the development of the conservation-of-energy law, which holds that the sum total of all energy in the universe remains constant.

Thomson's law became more important when the actual mechanical equivalent of heat was determined. This was done by James Prescott Joule, an amateur scientist who was a Manchester brewer by trade. After many experiments, he had obtained a result of 778 foot-pounds of work as the mechanical equivalent of the pound-degree Fahrenheit. *The Manchester Guardian* publicized his discovery, but the other English newspapers were not impressed. This did not matter to Joule, who realized that his work was potentially important. He succeeded in getting permission to read a paper about his discovery before the British Association at Oxford. Before the meeting, the chairman, thinking Joule's paper to be of little value, had advised him to be brief. Therefore Joule skimmed through his paper, and the little he did say was barely heard, because he was so nervous. (Thomson said later that "there was no consciousness in the very unassuming young man's manner that he had a great idea to unfold.") The chairman was about to pass on to another subject without asking for questions or further discussion, when Professor Thomson jumped to his feet. He asked the audience to consider how Joule's discovery might be used to determine the amount of energy changed to heat when an electric current flows through a wire. Today Joule's Laws are standards in thermodynamics.

Thomson was indebted to the research of Carnot and Joule for the clues that led him to develop his absolute temperature scale, which is independent of the properties of any thermometric substance and is used principally in thermodynamics. The Kelvin scale starts with the lowest possible temperature and calls it absolute zero. Since Thomson utilized centigrade divisions, the freezing point of water, or 0° centigrade, became 273° in his scale, and the boiling point of water, or 100° centigrade, became 373° Kelvin.

William Thomson was interested in all the scientific problems of his time, and inevitably he became involved in the development of telegraphic communication between England and America. In 1850 an experimental line had been laid across the English Channel between Dover and Calais. This cable was made of copper wire, insulated with the rubberlike substance, gutta-percha. In the try-out the signals received were characterized as "extraordinarily sluggish" and after a few hours, all communication ceased. The line had been severed by the anchor of a fishing smack. It would not be hard to make a stronger cable, but something had to be done to clarify the signals.

William Thomson knew that the cable was in effect an elongated Leyden jar of great capacity. The copper acted as the inner lining, the salt water as the outer lining, and the gutta-percha as the glass of the jar. When a battery is connected to one end of the core, the "Leyden jar" gradually gets charged up, first at the battery end, gradually farther and farther along the wire, and so to the other end. When the battery is withdrawn (or the circuit broken), the discharge is equally gradual.

Extending this principle, Thomson worked out a theory of the telegraph. The retardation of the electric impulse along a cable, he said, was proportional to the capacity and the resistance of the cable, and each of these quantities was proportional to the length to such an extent that the time retardation of a signal was in actual practice proportional to the square of the length. He illustrated: "If a cable 200 miles long showed a retardation of one-tenth of a second, one of similar thickness that was 2000 miles long would have a retardation 100 times as great, or ten seconds."

It seemed impossible to apply these proportions to

a cable long enough to cross the Atlantic, but Thomson had a solution. He said in effect: Employ a copper cable of the lowest resistance possible, and consequently of the highest conductivity, and use the thickest cross-section obtainable. There were many objections to his suggestion, but Thomson's reputation as a practical physicist was so great that plans were laid for the forming of the Atlantic Telegraph Company. Thomson himself was named chief director.

The cable was laid successfully but signals were so weak that ordinary receiving methods were useless. Thomson's solution was the invention of the mirror galvanometer, which is today considered an essential part of the equipment of every scientific laboratory. This instrument was quite simple. To the magnet at the center of the coil of an ordinary galvanometer Thomson attached a spherical mirror so that it hung vertically and swung with the magnet whenever a current passed around the coil. A spot of light from a lamp was reflected from this mirror to a distant scale. The scale was placed far enough away so that a tiny movement of the mirror caused a very noticeable swing of the spot along the scale. This instrument proved sensitive to even the smallest current changes and recorded very feeble currents.

More than seven hundred messages had been received and the problems presented by a transatlantic cable were apparently solved, when, suddenly, messages stopped coming. The cable had broken and it was impossible to mend it.

"We must build a new and better cable," said Thomson. He busied himself with the plans, arranging to have a cable ship, the *Great Eastern*, carry the whole length of cable required. He equipped the ship for the free maneuvering necessary to lay the cable. Two attempts were made before a successful line was laid in 1866. As electrical engineer of the expedition and the man most responsible for its success, William Thomson was knighted by Queen Victoria.

As time passed, Thomson found that his mirror galvanometer did not operate quite as efficiently as he wished. Eventually he replaced it with a siphon recorder. Part of this instrument was a small pen, made of glass tube and shaped like a siphon. One end of the pen dipped in an ink bottle, the other end wrote messages in little zigzag notches on a ribbon of paper drawn past it by machinery. The siphon-pen was moved by signal currents which flowed in a small coil hung between the poles of an electromagnet. The ink spurted from the pen to the paper in a succession of fine drops. This was done by electrifying the ink bottle and ink and keeping the paper in contact with an uninsulated metal roller. Attraction between the electrified ink and the unelectrified paper thus drew out the ink drops. Since the pen never touched paper, it was not retarded by friction.

While Thomson was working on transocean cables, he watched sailors repeat the inaccurate and time-consuming process of deep-sea sounding which was so important in laying cable. The ship would be stopped, a rope with a sinker at the end lowered into the ocean; then after it had reached bottom, it would be hauled up again and the paid-out line measured.

Thomson thought of a better way to measure the depth of the sea. He would use piano wire, which could be wound mechanically, and his sounder would be a glass tube, of small diameter, with the upper end stopped. The tube's interior would be coated with silver chromate, a chemical that changes color upon contact with salt water. When this tube was weighted and dropped into the sea, open end first, water pressure would increase as the tube sank to lower and lower depths. As the air trapped in the tube was increasingly compressed, more and more silver chromate would be exposed to the action of salt water. When Thomson's sounder was removed from the water, the ocean depth could be calculated from the height of discoloration on the tube.

Thomson had to experiment for a while before he perfected this invention. One day Joule found him surrounded with piano wire. When Joule asked what he was doing, Thomson replied, "Sounding."

"What note?" Joule asked, and Thomson promptly replied, "The deep *C*."

Today Thomson's sounding device, which has

evolved into a seven-strand steel cable three hundred fathoms in length, is still in use, and has saved countless ships from running aground. "Heave Thomson over!" commands the navigation officer whenever he wants to know the depth of the sea.

When Thomson was asked to write an article on the mariner's compass for a technical journal, he found that he knew very little about it. He studied the compasses then in use, and was surprised at how faulty they were. The needles were heavy, often fifteen inches long. They were mounted on large cards, supposedly to make them steady, but in fine weather they often stalled, and in stormy weather they were practically useless. After reading some studies of compass deviation, Thomson decided that a shorter needle mounted on a lighter card would be an improvement. "A slow horizontal swing will avoid unsteadiness," he said, "besides lessening the amount of friction to prevent sticking." He also realized that it was essential to shield a compass from the magnetism of the ship's ironwork. His improved mariner's compass was used almost universally until the advent of the gyrocompass.

Next Thomson turned his attention to lighthouses and suggested a system whereby one light could be distinguished from another. He made a study of the tides and a tide-predicting instrument. As a result of his mathematical investigation of waves, he made improvements in ship design. Thomson's fame reached such proportions that a sailor once said, "I don't know who this Thomson may be, but every sailor ought to pray for him every night."

In 1892, Queen Victoria raised Sir William to the peerage. He chose the title of Baron Kelvin of Largs, to perpetuate the name of the Kelvin River near Glasgow University. Honors from governments, scientific societies, and universities came to him from all over the world. He was president of the London Royal Society for five years, and of the Edinburgh Royal Society four times. In 1896 all Glasgow honored him for having completed a half-century as Professor of Natural Philosophy at the university. Representatives of many governments and scientific societies gathered to pay him homage.

Lord Kelvin remained at his university post for three years longer. Then, when he was seventy-five, he retired from his professorship. He was succeeded by Andrew Gray, a former student and assistant who later wrote a biography entitled *Lord Kelvin*.

Lord Kelvin by no means gave up his work when he retired from his professorship. On the very day of his resignation he enrolled as a special student in scientific research. For eight years longer he worked, hale and hearty "except for occasional bouts of facial neuralgia." He died on December 23, 1907, and was buried beside Sir Isaac Newton in Westminster Abbey. "There," says Andrew Gray, "he sleeps well who toiled during a long life for the cause of natural knowledge, and served nobly, as a hero of peace, his country and the world."

In May, 1921, scientists gathered at the Institute of Civil Engineers to award the newly created Kelvin Medal. In his speech on that occasion, Lord Balfour said:

Lord Kelvin had, in a manner hardly and perhaps never equaled before, except by Archimedes, the power of theorizing on the darkest, most obscure, and most intimate secrets of Nature, and at the same time, and almost in the same breath, carrying out effectively and practically some engineering feat, or carrying to a successful issue some engineering invention. He was one of the leaders in the movement which has compelled all modern engineers worthy of the name to be themselves men not merely of practice, but of theory, to carry out engineering undertakings in the spirit of true scientific inquiry and with an eye fixed on the rapidly growing knowledge of the mechanics of Nature, which can only be acquired by the patient work of physicists and mathematicians in their laboratories and studies.

CHAPTER 7

Thomas Alva Edison

Thomas Alva Edison was born into a country that was growing up fast. The railroad was pushing its way across the continent and the telegraph was just beginning its miraculous conquest of time and distance. Farmers were beginning to discard their sickles and scythes in favor of mowing machines and reapers. In a couple of years the California gold rush would open the West with a violent burst of activity. Industry was getting ready to tap our great resources of coal, iron, copper, and timber. Men who would be leading figures in this great new era were now children. Andrew Carnegie, for example, was a messenger boy in a telegraph office. It was a splendid time in which to be born.

Thomas Alva Edison was born on February 11, 1847 in Milan, Ohio, a great grain center. His great-grandfather had been the first of the Edison family to come to this country. He came from Holland to settle in New Jersey. During the War of Independence he was a bank official on Manhattan Island, and signed the Continental currency in 1778. He died at the age of one hundred and four. Thomas' grandfather, who died when he was one hundred and two, had originally migrated to Nova Scotia, but when he received a grant of six hundred acres on Lake Huron he moved there with wagon and oxen. Samuel Edison, Thomas' father, had taken part in the Canadian Rebellion of 1837. When the rebellion failed and the insurgents were being exiled to Bermuda, he fled with his wife through hostile Indian country to the United States.

The Edison family moved to Port Huron, a railroad town, when Thomas was young. As a child, Thomas was considered unusually inquisitive. From the time he was able to talk he asked questions all day long. In the shipyards he would ask the workmen what every single tool was used for. He would spend hours copying the signs from store fronts. At school he asked so many questions that the teacher thought this strange child with a small body and an unusually large head must be "addled." She told his mother so. But Mrs. Edison was an intelligent woman, who had been a teacher herself. Realizing that Thomas' curiosity needed sympathetic direction, she tutored him at home. By the time he was nine, he had read Gibbon's *Decline and Fall of the Roman Empire* and Burton's *Anatomy of Melancholy.*

To Edison his experiments were the most important of his activities. Perhaps his first was one he performed at the age of six. His parents found him in the barn sitting on a nest of eggs; he had seen how a goose hatched her eggs, and he wanted to try the same thing himself. When he was seven, he set fire to his father's barn "to see what it would do." It "did" a great deal. It burned to the ground, and young Thomas was whipped in public.

For a long time he had had a chemical laboratory in the cellar. There were rows and rows of bottles, every one marked: "Poison—Don't Touch." He made his pocket money by selling vegetables from the garden, but now he decided that he needed more money to finance his laboratory. So, with his parents' consent, he became a newsboy and candy vendor on the Detroit–Port Huron trains, a job which kept him away from home from seven in the morning to ten at night.

Before long Thomas had two stores in Port Huron, which he paid other boys to run. Meanwhile he had bought some type and started his own newspaper. The *Weekly Herald* reached a circulation of eight hundred. Edison stimulated its sale by telegraphing ahead bits of news to the stations along the way. People read these incomplete bulletins, then bought his papers as soon as they arrived. The paper netted him forty-five dollars a month. Altogether he earned two thousand dollars in four years.

Edison's headquarters were in a part of the train's

baggage car that was never used. There he had his printing press, his shelves of bottles, and all the miscellane-
ous apparatus he had collected. One day something
happened which put an end to his enterprises on the
railway. A bottle of phosphorus broke on the floor and
set the car on fire. At the next station, the conductor
put Edison off the train, throwing his printing press,
type, and chemicals after him onto the platform.

While this ended his traveling chemical laboratory, another interest soon proved absorbing. His visits
to telegraph offices had aroused his enthusiasm for
electricity and the telegraph. It was not long before he
and a friend had set up a crude line of communication
between their two houses. It worked—even though it
was made out of old stove pipe, wire, and bottle necks.

Now a fortunate accident helped further Edison's
career. He was standing one day with a bundle of papers
under his arm talking with the station agent at Mount
Clemens station. Suddenly he caught sight of a child
playing on the track where a train was backing in. He
darted out after the child and carried him to safety. In
gratitude, the station agent—who was the child's father
—offered to teach Edison how to be a telegraph operator. After a short period of instruction, Edison applied
for a job as operator at Port Huron. He got the position
at twenty-five dollars a month.

Edison undoubtedly was brilliant, but he was a
far from dependable operator. If he was absorbed in a
book, telegrams waited until he was through. He lit-

tered the place with chemicals and apparatus. His employer was understandably annoyed. The last straw came when Edison was discovered sleeping during night duty. Night operators were naturally supposed to stay awake, and do their sleeping in the daytime. To prove they were not sleeping on the job, they were obliged to send to the central office each hour the expression "six."

Since Edison could not bear to waste daylight in sleep, he invented a device which he attached to the clock. The invention sent the signal automatically every hour. It worked fine until the supervisor decided to "call him up" over the telegraph for a little chat. He began sending. There was no answer, although the signal "six" had just come through. Deciding that something had gone wrong, he went up the tracks on a handcar to find out. There he discovered the sixteen-year-old operator fast asleep. The supervisor could not resist the temptation of waiting till the time for the next signal. Then he saw Edison's invention do its work. But there was no denying that Edison was neglecting his duties, so he was discharged at once.

At his next post, he got into a worse scrape. This was in Sarnia, a town across the river in Canada. Again he went to sleep on the job, nearly causing a serious train wreck. Edison left that job in a hurry.

Edison spent the next four years as a roving operator. Because of the Civil War there was a great demand for telegraphers, so it was an easy matter to drift from one town to another, picking up jobs on the way. He worked in Indianapolis, Cincinnati, Memphis, Louisville. Throughout all his wandering he read constantly. With his spare money he bought books in auction rooms and secondhand shops. Once, in Detroit, he decided that the way to become educated was to start at the top shelf in the library and read each book in turn. After wading through fifteen feet of books he gave up.

When he was twenty-one, Edison returned to Port Huron, somewhat the worse for wear. Fortunately he received an offer to go to Boston to work for Western Union. There the other telegraph employees thought his shoddy clothes a great joke, and made a good deal of fun of him—until they found that he was an expert telegrapher.

Edison continued experimenting just as enthusiastically as ever—and with the usual unfortunate results. He made some gun cotton and it blew up the stove. He spilled sulphuric acid over his new clothes. Even his invention for the electrocution of cockroaches got him into trouble. This contrivance made a great hit when it was installed, but its very popularity caused its downfall. Admiring reporters played up the story in the local papers, but Edison's superiors were highly indignant at seeing Western Union cockroaches featured by the press.

Edison's career to date had not been marked by

conspicuous success. Suddenly, however, at the age of twenty-one, he changed from an experimenter to an inventor.

The first invention which he patented was the Electric Vote Recorder, intended for use among legislative bodies. With this recorder there would be no necessity for counting noses, since "ayes" and "noes" would be recorded automatically at the Speaker's desk. Edison went all the way to Washington to get it adopted, sure that his fortune was made. He failed to realize that delay occasioned by vote-counting is just what the minority likes. Acceptance was out of the question. But, while Edison's first patented invention was a dismal failure, it may have been one of his most important. Edison himself said afterwards, "It got me to the point of giving up practical telegraphy."

He was never again to be an operator, for from now on his fortune changed almost like magic. Borrowing some money, he took the night boat for New York. It was during the depression that followed the Civil War, and although he secured promise of work with Western Union, he had to wait for an opening. He nearly starved while waiting.

Edison secured permission to sleep in the battery-room of the Gold Indicator Company. This room had been established in Wall Street for gold speculators, as paper money had depreciated. There was a system of about three hundred indicators in the offices of brokers, and these indicators were operated from a complicated transmitting instrument at the Exchange, each showing the price fluctuations as transactions took place. Edison studied the complicated transmitting instrument, which was controlled from the keyboard of the operator on the floor of the Gold Exchange. In that day, fluctuations in the price of gold might mean instant ruin, or fortune. On Edison's third day there, the noisy instruments suddenly crashed in silence. At once three hundred boys, one from every broker in the street, rushed up yelling that So-and-so's wire was out of order. The man in charge got so excited he was useless. Edison found the trouble. One of the contact springs had broken off and fallen into the apparatus. He fixed it, then showed the President of the Exchange, Dr. S. S. Laws, how he could simplify things. Dr. Laws put Edison in charge of the plant, at $300 a month. Edison promptly began putting twenty hours a day into the work, devising improvements.

While waiting for a train late one night, he invented an instrument to print gold quotations instead of indicating them. It was called the Universal Printer. General Marshall Lefferts, president of the Gold and Stock Telegraph Company, offered to buy Edison's invention. Edison scarcely dared to ask $5,000 for it. When the General offered him $40,000, he was dumbfounded. As a practical joke, the bank tellers gave him a cubic foot of small bills for his check. Edison stuffed them in his pockets, sitting up all night with them before he opened his first bank account.

Edison was now independent, and could devote his entire time to his inventions. At once he bought machinery and opened a factory in Newark. Building stock tickers to start with, he soon had a force of a hundred and fifty men, and was so busy that he allowed himself only half an hour's sleep three or four times in the twenty-four hours. One of his employees was Sigmund Bergmann, later a partner in the Edison lighting developments, and eventually head of a mammoth electrical works in Berlin. Another employee was John Kruesi, who later became engineer of the General Electrical Works at Schenectady. There was also Schuckert, later founder of the Nuremberg electrical factory, third largest in Germany.

Busy days followed. Edison had no less than forty-five separate inventions under way. His laboratory notebooks record literally thousands of experiments made at this time. He was keenly interested in multiple transmission, and devised a way of sending two messages simultaneously over one wire, first in opposite directions, then in the same direction. The first was called duplex and the second, diplex. With his quadruplex system, which was a logical development of the systems already mentioned, he was able to send, simultaneously, two messages in opposite directions. The quadruplex system is estimated to have saved about twenty million dollars in the cost of line construction in the United States.

Though Bell had invented a telephone, the sounds

produced were weak. Curiously enough, Edison had filed a description of his own telephone on January 14, 1876, a month before Bell filed his application for a patent. Edison's first telephone was not for transmitting speech; he devised it merely for analyzing the complicated waves that arose from various sounds. Edison always gave Bell full credit for the discovery of transmitting articulate speech in an electric current. But Bell's telephone was practicable for short lines only, and the public considered it little better than a try. Western Union asked Edison to make a telephone that would be commercially useful.

The thing that made the telephone really practicable was the carbon transmitter. This Edison patented in 1877. Inside the mouthpiece was a mica diaphragm, and between two small platinum disks was a quantity of compressed lampblack. An ivory button on the front disk made contact with the mica diaphragm, on which the sound waves dashed. The steady direct current passing through the carbon granules of the lampblack was made to fluctuate in step with the sound waves striking the diaphragm.

Edison put in months of work, employing a corps of helpers, before he completed the invention of this carbon transmitter, together with his plan of using an induction coil and a constant battery current on the line. The millions of telephones in use today bear the imprint of these principles.

Western Union later offered Edison $100,000—

five times what he had meant to ask for the invention. Remembering the days when he had actually gone hungry, Edison asked that it be paid at the rate of $6,000 a year for seventeen years—the life of the patent. He afterward said he saved himself seventeen years of worry by that stroke.

When Edison first dreamed of an incandescent electric light, newspapers called him a madman. Early experimenters had worked on a lamp of a kind that would have cost a fortune to operate because it required an enormous outlay of copper. Edison decided to try a "glow lamp" requiring a small quantity of current, one that possessed only a small radiating surface. His experiments revolved around the fact that in passing through any substance a current meets with resistance. A very thin wire, which offers high resistance, may be raised to a white heat and so made to glow with light. Edison's first concern was to find a substance that could be formed into a fine filament that could be kept in a state of incandescence without melting. Such a filament had to have a suitable surface for radiating light, yet the substance must not be too good a conductor or heating it would require currents too large and expensive. Neither must the filament be too long and fine.

He first tried platinum, which is not acted upon by gases in the air. His earliest lamps contained spirals of thin platinum wire, each sealed in a glass bulb from which the air had been exhausted. Experiments showed that when platinum was kept continuously at a high temperature it quickly disintegrated, and Edison's platinum lamps had so short a life that they were of no practical value.

He then tried using fine filaments of carbon, which were more durable than platinum and a very great deal cheaper. At that time carbon had been experimented with, but not with such results as would produce a light that could be sold to the public at a reasonable price. Edison dreamed of a lamp with a tough hairlike filament, a light-giving body that could be maintained at a white heat for perhaps a thousand hours without breaking.

Carbon is a substance offering resistance to electricity so that it glows when a current is on. It is low in cost, and did not melt at any temperature Edison had as yet attained. It seemed to him the best material for use as a filament in electric lamps. Edison found, however, that it would combine with oxygen in the air and burn out. It was thus imperative to exclude air from the bulb of the incandescent lamp. Working night and day, Edison and his associates at Menlo Park, New Jersey, where he had built research laboratories, evolved a one-piece, all-glass globe, hermetically sealed. On October 21, 1879, he carbonized a piece of cotton thread bent into a loop and had it sealed into a glass globe from which he exhausted the air. This lamp was put on the electric circuit, and it lighted up to incandescence, lasting forty hours. Edison watched it intently during the entire period.

He now began experimenting with every substance he could think of, from cork to coconut fiber. He tested six thousand varieties of vegetable growth to find the ideal filament. In those days palm-leaf fans were much used in summer. Edison was handling a broken fan when it occurred to him to try a filament from the bamboo bound around the edge of the fan. The results were so excellent that he sent men to South America and the Orient to find the best varieties of bamboo for his purpose. In all, Edison studied twelve hundred kinds of bamboo. At last he decided upon a specimen grown in Japan and hired a Japanese farmer to grow this bamboo and ship it regularly to the laboratory. Millions of the early electric lamps were made with filaments of that bamboo.

On New Year's Eve, 1879, he showed the world incandescent electric lighting from a central station. Having given the world improved electric lighting, he next devised a system by which electric light, heat, and power might be distributed from a central powerhouse. This involved a network of conductors, a means of measuring electricity by meter, efficient dynamos, devices to prevent fire from excessive current, and even provision for switches and lamp holders, to complete the system. It was the beginning of a great industry. By the end of 1880 the Edison Electric Light Company was renting offices in a mansion at 65 Fifth Avenue, New York. Edison and his associates had invented all the apparatus manufactured. He had also trained men to use it. In 1881 the electric lighting of his office building was a sight to draw thousands. Then came a rush of business that was phenomenal. The first lamps cost $1.25 each for bulbs, and Edison set out to get the cost down. When he had the bulb selling for forty cents, Wall Street investors bought him out for over a million dollars.

When Edison invented something, the process of inventing it usually did not take long. One day, in 1877, he invented the phonograph. He was toying with the carbon transmitter of a telephone, singing into the mouthpiece. The needle point which is a part of the mechanism, vibrating from the sound of his voice, suddenly pricked his finger. Edison decided that this same needle point could transfer sound vibrations onto some recording substance. He quickly sketched plans for a working model. One of his assistants took the drawings and did not come back until the instrument was completed. He set it down in front of Edison, somewhat amused and rather skeptical. The model itself was certainly nothing to look at. It consisted of a base, a cylinder, a crank, and some gadgets. The workers in the shop gathered around. Although they were used to Edison's "miracles," none of them thought the machine would work. Carman, the shop foreman, bet Edison a box of cigars it wouldn't. Without saying a word, Edison covered the cylinder with tinfoil. Turning the crank, he recited "Mary had a little lamb" into the strange machine. The workmen gathered closer around the table. Edison turned the crank again, and his voice came back to them—unmistakable. Carman handed Edison a cigar and walked out of the room.

Edison's "talking machine" was considered by many to be a great hoax. Investigations were started, and crowds swarmed out to Menlo Park. The Pennsylvania Railroad had to run special trains to accommodate the curious.

It was a long road from Edison's first crank and cylinder machine to the modern phonograph. Edison made machine after machine. Fifty of them in all were made and destroyed, one after the other. Before the modern talking machine was finished, two million dollars had been spent.

To the generations that have never known what it was to be without electric lights, the movies may seem to be Edison's greatest achievement. Before he was born there had been a toy called the "Wheel of Life" or "Zoetrope." One of the wonders to be seen at every country fair, it contained a succession of tiny pictures which, revolving swiftly on a cylinder, seemed to be moving figures. It worked because of "persistence of vision," that is, because the human eye holds an image for a fraction of a second after the object viewed has been removed. Edison wondered why, with innumerable photographs, you could not produce large-scale series of moving pictures. The big question was how to get the proper kind of camera to take these countless pictures, to say nothing of the proper kind of film. Dry plates were in common use, but a motion picture lasting only fifteen minutes requires more than sixteen thousand separate photographs. Obviously dry plates would never do. Edison conferred with George Eastman of the Eastman Kodak Company. While the film was being perfected, he set up his photographic laboratory. He was convinced that he could produce a mechanism which would do for the eye what the phonograph had already done for the ear.

In due course, Edison created the kinetoscope, the forerunner of the modern moving picture projector. Eastman manufactured suitable film, and before long they were "shooting" short pictures and novelties in the laboratory. Edison even predicted "talkies," for he said at this time that the day would come when operas would be seen and heard long after the singers were dead.

During his career, Edison patented 1,099 separate inventions. He worked so fast that he confused the patent office. In a period of four years he produced three hundred inventions. It is estimated that commerce owes 7,000 billion dollars a year to enterprises which first originated in his extraordinary brain. He could have retired with a fortune as a very young man. Instead, he continued to work and kept a cot in his laboratory so that he might rest sometimes during his long working day.

In 1931 he died, and some seven years later a memorial tower and light was built in Menlo Park. In

Greenfield village in Dearborn, Michigan, his Menlo Park workshop and one of his laboratories have been preserved, due to the efforts of Henry Ford. Edison's particular genius was not so much in abstract science as it was in the application of scientific principles, and in almost every area of modern industry the effects of that genius may be seen.

CHAPTER 8

Marie and Pierre Curie

In 1920 three hundred men dug in southern Colorado for a yellow sand called "carnotite." They hauled it eighteen roadless miles to a concentration mill where five hundred tons became one hundred tons. Then they shipped it in sacks to Canonsburg, Pennsylvania. By the time another two hundred men had boiled, filtered, and crystallized it, using tons of coal and tons of acids, a few crystals of a magic salt remained, a gram which had cost $100,000 to produce. This gram of radium, representing a year's work, was presented by the President of the United States, acting in the name of one hundred thousand American women, to Marie Curie, discoverer of the element.

With the help of her husband, Mme. Curie had performed the actual labor necessary to obtain the world's first gram of radium. She had conceived the idea that there might be such an element, as yet undiscovered. And she and her husband were largely responsible for the use of radium as a curative agent.

Marie Curie was born in Warsaw on November 7, 1867, daughter of Vladislav Sklodovski, a professor of physics and mathematics. Her mother was also a teacher. Marie's parents were members of the lesser nobility, whose fortunes had been ruined with those of their country, Poland, part of which at that time was subject to Russia.

The director of the school where Marie's father taught was one of the agents of the Russian Czar. These agents were called "russificators"; they saw to it that the Polish people made no move toward freedom, spoke no Polish in their schools and churches, and rebelled only at the cost of joining a chain gang in Siberia. Polish children never knew, as they chatted on their way home from school, but that any casual passer-by might be a Russian spy ready to report their conversations, and they were trained to be as cautious as their elders, who still hoped for the freedom of Poland.

Because he would not be servile to the headmaster, Professor Sklodovski was demoted to a post where his salary was entirely inadequate. By the time Marie was eight, her mother was dying of tuberculosis, her father had had to take in a houseful of students to board and tutor, and her eldest sister had died of typhus. Her mother died two years later, when Marie was ten.

Marie was a brilliant student; her father tutored her at home in the evenings. Joseph and Bronya, her older brother and sister, were awarded gold medals when they left high school. Joseph went on to study medicine at the University of Warsaw, but Bronya, because she was a girl, was not allowed to enter. Marie attended a Russian high school, which was run with rigid discipline. She, too, won a gold medal for being the best student in her class.

Although Professor Sklodovski could not afford to send Marie and Bronya to college, the girls did not give up hope. They wanted to go to the Sorbonne, an international center of learning in Paris, where Marie could train as a teacher and Bronya study medicine, a six-year course. The sisters made a plan: first Marie would find a position as a tutor and send some of her wages to Bronya to help pay her expenses at the Sorbonne. Later Bronya would in turn help Marie.

So Marie then became governess for a well-to-do family who lived on an estate outside Warsaw. She remained with them three years, marking the days and faithfully sending most of her salary to Bronya. During this time, the eldest son in the family fell in love with Marie, who was strikingly pretty, danced well, and was fun to talk to. Marie also was infatuated, but his parents, her employers, opposed their son's marriage to a lowly governess. Marie could not afford to leave her job; she stayed on although now her relations with her employers were bitter and strained.

At last, when Marie was twenty-four, Bronya wrote that she was going to be married, that she would soon be finished with her education, and would be able to help her sister. Now Marie could begin the education she longed for. Before very long, she had moved into a barren attic room, the first of a series of cheap lodgings where for three years she existed on little more than buttered bread and tea to cut down the expenses and also because she had no interest in food. She had discovered her lifework, science, and cared for nothing else. She had never been happier.

When Marie was twenty-seven, she was introduced to a tall, lean physicist named Pierre Curie, who was head of a large laboratory and doing graduate work at the Sorbonne. Although he was thirty-five, he appeared young to her and she liked his "simplicity and his smile." Pierre was almost as preoccupied with his work as Marie was with her studies, but not too preoccupied to fall in love with the graceful young Pole, who understood his most obscure scientific language and liked nothing better than to listen to it. He asked her to marry him, or at least to work in his laboratory. Marie was happy to accept the job but waited awhile to accept the proposal.

In July of 1895, Pierre and Marie were married. For a wedding trip, they rode off on two new bicycles and spent the nights at any inn they came to. Sometimes they parked their bicycles and went for long walks through the beautiful French countryside. Pierre loved to hike; he often had good ideas about his work when he was walking. Toward the end of summer, the Curies stayed for a while on a farm near Chantilly, where some of Marie's relatives joined them. In the fall the couple returned to Paris, settled down in a tiny apartment, and resumed their careers.

Pierre was now teaching at the School of Physics in the Sorbonne, but his income was small. After a while Marie, too, began to teach. She continued to work under Pierre at the laboratory. In addition she prepared meals, laundered, sewed, and marketed—as she continued to do for many years to come. She had never learned to cook, and she set about it with great seriousness and scientific care as if it were a difficult laboratory problem. In the evenings she studied for a fellowship competition. When she won it, passing first on the list, she and Pierre celebrated with a bicycle trip through Auvergne.

In September, 1897, the Curies' first child was born —Irène, who was later also to become a physicist and a Nobel Prize winner. Marie felt no conflict between her responsibilities as mother and wife and her work. She was determined to do everything and do it well, and not long after Irène was born, Marie began her major scientific work.

In January, 1896, Roentgen had discovered X-rays, which could penetrate solid objects and show the bony skeleton in the living body. Henri Poincaré had raised the question: Were rays like those of the X-ray emitted by "fluorescent bodies under the action of light?" Becquerel, who was doing research in an attempt to answer this question, accidentally left a piece of uranium ore upon a sensitized plate in his workroom and found the plate had been affected, even in the absence of visible light. He had discovered the phenomenon that Marie Curie later named "radioactivity."

At this time Marie Curie had two university degrees. She had written a monograph on the magnetization of tempered steel, and she was considering a subject on which to base her research for a doctor's degree. She had been impressed by the work of Becquerel, and was curious about the rays emitted spontaneously by uranium salts.

Marie conducted her first experiments in the only place at the university that was available—a tiny studio in the School of Physics where the temperature was sometimes as low as six degrees. There she was first to measure the power of ionization of uranium rays, that is, their power to make the air a conductor of electricity and thus discharge an electroscope. The method she used had been invented by her husband and his brother Jacques Curie.

After a few weeks Marie concluded that the intensity of radiation was proportional to the amount of uranium in her samples, and that the radiation was not affected by uranium's combinations with other chemicals or by such external factors as temperature and light.

Marie wondered whether uranium was the *only*

element that emitted radiation. To find the answer, she began to test every known chemical, both elements and compounds. She discovered that compounds of another element, thorium, also emitted rays like those of uranium. Then Marie named thorium and uranium "radioactive elements," because they emitted rays unceasingly.

Her search had only begun. She continued to test salts, oxides, and minerals until one day she found something that was hard to explain. She tested a radioactive ore, an ore that she knew contained both uranium and thorium. But the sum of the ore's radioactivity was greater than its known radioactive parts! On April 12, 1898, she announced that there probably existed in pitchblende ores "a new element gifted with powerful radioactivity." Now her task was to find it.

Pierre Curie left his own research in the spring of 1898 to help Marie in her search for the new element. During the next four years, the Curies worked together in the only place the university would give them—a leaky shed in the courtyard outside Marie's old office. Formerly, it had been used for dissection. Now it was not even adequate for storing cadavers. "In our poor shed there reigned a great tranquility," Marie wrote. ". . . We lived in our single preoccupation as if in a dream."

As the Curies removed the uranium and inert material from pitchblende, their sample became smaller and smaller; but at the same time the radioactivity of what was left kept increasing. Finally, in the residue, Marie discovered infinitesimal traces of the new element, which was both rare and radioactive. She called it "polonium" after her native Poland.

Not content with their discovery of one new element, the Curies began to search for another, which they had reason to believe was also contained in pitchblende and was even more radioactive than polonium. They worked with tons of ore, hoping that from such a large quantity they would be able to isolate enough of their new element to prove its existence—enough to see, weigh, and study chemically.

After years of separating, extracting, and concentrating, they isolated a decigram of what looked like table salt but had extraordinary properties. They had discovered a compound of a new element—radium. The salts of radium glowed in the dark; they continually gave off heat; the radium in the compound was millions of times more radioactive than uranium. How the new element could be isolated from its compound, and what its uses would be, were not yet known.

The Curies were handicapped by a lack of money. In 1898 Pierre had been offered a chair of physics at the University of Geneva. Although the salary was tempting, he and Marie chose to remain where they were and continue their research. They took on additional teaching jobs to pay their living expenses and to buy scientific equipment.

As they continued to study radium, they found

that the ends of their fingers were affected by it. It was Pierre Curie who made one of the first tests that led to the discovery of radium's power to cure. Deliberately exposing his arm to the element, he received a burn and recorded the progress of his wound with scientific detachment. Then he used laboratory animals to learn more about the biological effects of radioactivity. Eventually, through the research of other scientists, as well as the Curies', it was discovered that radium, by destroying diseased cells, cured tumors and certain kinds of cancer. The term "Curietherapy" was coined, and Marie and Pierre lent tubes of radium to French physicians.

When a factory was built to produce the element for medical use, Marie and Pierre taught technicians the delicate processes of radium separation.

Radium had other interesting properties. It made diamonds highly phosphorescent, changed its colorless glass containers to violet, and caused the atmosphere to conduct electricity. It made everything in the laboratory somewhat radioactive.

To obtain the first gram of radium, the Curies, mainly Marie, treated eight tons of pitchblende. At this time they could have sold their gram for $150,000, but they decided to keep it for further study. They did not even patent their invention to assure themselves of an income, for Marie thought that would be "contrary to the scientific spirit," and Pierre agreed.

France was slow to recognize the Curies' achievement, but other nations were not. In 1903 the Royal Institution of Great Britain invited Pierre to lecture and the Royal Society of London awarded the Curies the Davy Medal. Later that year the Curies and Henri Becquerel won the Nobel Prize in physics for their combined discoveries about radioactivity. The seventy thousand francs the Curies received was especially welcome, since it enabled them to hire a laboratory assistant. Later the Osiris Prize brought them fifty thousand francs. With it Marie made gifts to her family, to an old teacher, and to some Polish students. She also insisted that Pierre leave the School of Physics, because his health was poor. As they continued their work, fame seemed to mean chiefly an invasion of their home life by reporters. When the Curies went to the country on their brief vacations, they used to register at obscure country inns under assumed names.

The University of Paris finally created a chair of physics for Pierre. Marie, now thirty-six, continued to teach. She bought a little place in the valley of Chevreuse, near Paris, and here her second daughter was born—Eve who, when she grew up, wrote *Madame Curie,* the thrilling story of her mother's life.

On Easter Sunday, 1906, Pierre and Marie spent a day in the country. On the following Thursday, when Pierre was walking in a congested Paris street, he was run down by a horse-drawn wagon and instantly killed. Contrary to tradition, the Sorbonne offered Marie the professorship left vacant by her husband. She was to be the first woman ever to have such a post at the famous university. At half-past one on a day in November, she walked onto the platform and resumed Pierre's last lecture at the precise sentence where he had ended.

Thereafter, for thirty years, she carried on the research they had begun together. To build the laboratory of which Pierre had dreamed, a laboratory where the science of radioactivity could be developed, became the object of her life.

For a time she did her research alone. Then, in 1910, collaborating with André Debierne, she isolated radium in a pure form for the first time. To do this, she first passed an electric current through molten radium chloride, noting a chemical change at the negative mercury electrode. An amalgam was forming. She heated the alloy in a silica tube filled with nitrogen under reduced pressure, the mercury boiled off in vapor, and there at last lay the brilliant white globules of pure metallic radium.

It was one of the most difficult experiments ever done and for it, in 1911, Marie Curie was again awarded a Nobel Prize. She was offered the Cross of Chevalier of the Legion of Honor, but declined it because Pierre had once declined his. She was also nominated for the august French Academy, but missed being elected by one vote—because she was a woman. In 1913 she founded a radium institute in Warsaw.

When the First World War began, Mme. Curie trained her daughter, Irène, who was seventeen, and a hundred and fifty other young girls to become X-ray technicians. In order to get equipment to the front, so that wounded men might be X-rayed, she devised a "radiological car" (called a "little Curie") equipped with Roentgen apparatus and a dynamo driven by the motor of the car. Mme. Curie learned to drive the first of over twenty such cars herself and personally saw to it that aid was carried to the wounded close behind the lines. Once, when it looked as if the Germans might reach Paris, she took her precious gram of radium to Bordeaux where she put it in a safety deposit box. She also installed two hundred radiological rooms in hospitals, and over a million wounded men were examined by X-ray.

There was now in Paris an Institute of Radium, or rather, two institutes under one roof, one a laboratory of radioactivity under the direction of Marie Curie, the other a laboratory for curietherapy and biological research in the treatment of cancer, organized by Professor Claude Regaud.

In 1921 Mme. Curie visited the United States, where Yale, Wellesley, Smith, Columbia, St. Lawrence, Pennsylvania, and the University of Chicago awarded her honorary degrees. When asked what she would like best in the world, she replied, "A gram of radium that would be mine to use." There were, by this time, a hundred and fifty grams in the world, but not one gram in Poland. Marie Curie wanted Poland to have one gram and her own laboratory another. It was to fulfill this wish that the women of America contributed funds to give her a second gram of radium.

When Mme. Curie returned to France, she kept to her usual exhausting schedule at the Radium Institute, combining administrative work and teaching with scientific research. In the spring of 1934 she became gravely ill. Doctors were puzzled by her condition, which was unfamiliar to them; gradually she grew weaker. Early in the morning of July 4, 1934, Marie Curie died; tests of her blood revealed the fundamental cause: her bone marrow had been damaged by the radioactive substances with which she had worked for so many years.

"Madame Curie," commented her friend, Professor Regaud, "can be counted among the eventual victims of the radioactive bodies which she and her husband discovered."

CHAPTER 9

Guglielmo Marconi

When the first wireless signal—three dots, the letter S—sputtered across the Atlantic Ocean in 1901, people at last recognized that the work of twenty-seven-year-old Guglielmo Marconi was important.

Before this it had been conceded that Marconi might be able to send a few signals back and forth across the English Channel. It was even acknowledged that a British ship, two hundred and fifty miles off shore, once had picked up a wireless flash. But how could mariners, or anyone else, seriously believe that messages could be consistently picked up out of the air from remote distances? Scientists, who certainly knew more than a boy inventor, had proved on paper the absurdity of the idea. The curvature of the earth, they said, made it impossible to send these "waves" very far. Relaying messages without wires was foolish.

Marconi had ignored their skepticism. He began his great experiment in transatlantic telegraphy with the construction of a transmitting aerial at Poldhu, a point on the southwestern coast of England that juts out into the Atlantic. For eleven months he and his men worked, erecting a ring of twenty wooden masts, each one two hundred feet high. But the job was hardly done when a coastal storm blew them all down.

Marconi immediately put up another aerial suspended on two poles. A preliminary signal sent over this aerial was picked up in Ireland. This was the first step of Marconi's experiment.

The same month, Marconi sailed for Newfoundland with two assistants, ready for the second step. In their baggage they had several balloons and a lot of large kites. Marconi realized that constructing suitable aerial towers on the stormy coast of Newfoundland would be a prodigious job. Instead of setting up towers for the aerial, he intended to let the wind help him carry out his plans.

He selected Signal Hill, across the bay from St. John's, and one windy morning began the experiment. The first balloon lifted the ten-pound aerial high in the air, but before long it tore loose and blew out to sea. The next day he released a kite in a high wind, and soon had it flying four hundred feet in the air. Everything was ready for the test.

Marconi's station at Poldhu was to signal constantly from 11:30 to 2:30, St. John's time. But Marconi was uncertain how to tune in on the signals, for no wave meter had been invented yet.

For half an hour Marconi sat at his receiving apparatus—a crude coherer type of instrument, a battery, and a telephone receiver—listening intently without hearing a thing. Then, suddenly, he heard three little clicks in the receiver. They were faint, but there they were, coming again and again.

For three days Marconi made no announcement, waiting to be sure he was right. When at last he revealed what had occurred, *The New York Times* ran a front-page story. It began: "St. John's, N.F., Dec. 14. —Guglielmo Marconi announced tonight the most wonderful scientific development of recent times."

Marconi, his belief in wireless vindicated, became the hero of the hour. Reporters besieged him, and scientists deluged him with congratulations.

It is hard for us to understand the struggle which attended the birth of wireless telegraphy. It has become so much a part of our lives that it is commonplace. What began as the "wireless"—an invention enabling ships' operators to signal each other in dots and dashes with headphones and sending key—has now been developed into radio and television.

But toward the end of the last century such means of communication were still in the realm of science fiction. Scientists had not yet solved the electromagnetic puzzle. Among those who were working on it were the experts William Preece, Oliver Lodge, and Augusto Righi. Edison, Kelvin, and Branly were interested on-lookers.

But electromagnetism baffled them all. There were all sorts of theories, prophecies, and scraps of information; and there had been some interesting experiments. Morse had been able to send a message through a river without direct wires, using the water as a conductor. In 1880, John Trowbridge even suggested a theoretical system of wireless communication, but nothing ever came of it. Several years later a Professor Dolbear managed to send signals over half a mile without using wires. But he believed it was air that furnished the connection.

It remained for someone to figure out exactly which facts and discoveries were important, someone to fit the puzzle together.

Added together, the discoveries of three different men in three different countries gave the answer.

1. James Clerk Maxwell, in England, demonstrated by mathematical reasoning that electromagnetic waves exist. He contended that these waves shoot through space with the speed of light. He did not, however, generate any such waves himself or discover how to detect them.

2. Heinrich Rudolph Hertz, in Germany, noticed that if an electric spark were made to jump a gap, it seemed to send impulses for a short distance, without any wires. He not only produced these Hertzian, or

radio, waves, but discovered how to detect them and measure their lengths.

3. Edouard Branly, in France, developed a detector or "coherer." This was a tube in which metal filings would cling together as a result of a near-by electrical charge. In other words, he devised a means by which the electrical impulses could be picked up.

These three important steppingstones enabled Marconi, then a boy of twenty, to begin developing long-distance wireless telegraphy.

Young Marconi could hardly be called a trained scientist. He never went to public school or to a university. Because his health was not good when he was a boy, his childhood was lonely. Although he enjoyed riding and swimming, he kept to himself most of the time, and had few boyhood friends.

Marconi's father was a wealthy Italian businessman, who lived in Bologna. His mother was Irish, and came from a family of Dublin distillers. Because of his poor health, Guglielmo had a tutor and spent most of his boyhood on the family estate at Pontecchio. He read a great deal, especially about chemistry, and made experiments in collecting atmospheric nitrates. He also studied steam engines and electricity, and Benjamin Franklin's experiments with static. Once he built an apparatus made of zinc on the roof of the house. It resembled a spear and was wired so that a bell would ring when enough static electricity had collected.

When Guglielmo was seven, he entered a school

in Florence, where he studied each winter. One of his courses was physics, and when still a schoolboy, he became interested in the puzzling electric impulses known as Hertzian waves. He decided that an important distinction should be made between Hertzian waves and ordinary electric currents. The waves produced by a spark would have the faculty of traveling without wires. Ordinary electric currents, however, traveled through a wire or some conductor. Guglielmo pointed out the difference in an illustration that became famous: Until a bell is struck it produces no sound; but when it is hit with a hammer, it transmits sound waves in every direction. The spark is the hammer blow; the sound waves the Hertzian oscillations.

When Guglielmo was twenty, he and his brother Luigi spent their vacation at Biellese, in the Italian Alps. One day he was reading in a scientific magazine about the work of Hertz, who had just died. The article told how Hertz sent electric waves across a room and was able to detect their presence by a spark produced in the gap of a small loop of wire. Marconi decided that Hertzian waves could be sent across the ocean just as well as they could be sent across a room. He spent the rest of his vacation drawing plans and diagrams.

As soon as they returned to Pontecchio he started to work in an attic laboratory where his father used to store silk cocoons. He worked for more than a month to produce a mechanism that would transmit Hertzian waves a few feet and record them. His first attempts failed, but after more weeks of experiment, he was so sure of success that he invited his parents to witness the results of his work.

Marconi pressed a button on the third floor. This time he succeeded in ringing an unconnected bell on the ground floor. Several days later he increased the intervening distance, and repeated the performance on the front lawn.

Marconi's father was so impressed by his son's achievement that he gave Guglielmo 5,000 lire ($1,000) with which to conduct further experiments.

The Italian government was not enthusiastic about the invention. When Marconi offered it to his country, it was refused. He then decided that England, a great naval power, would probably be more receptive. Besides, he had connections there. When he was seven, his cousin Jameson Davis had visited Italy. Davis was now an engineer living in London.

But Marconi's first encounter with the English was not promising. When he arrived in England, the customs authorities thought that his instruments looked suspicious and smashed them up. However, Marconi's luck changed when, at his cousin's home, he met Sir William Preece, to whom he had a letter of introduction. Sir William not only offered Marconi his own laboratory, he also used his influence to help the young inventor. In December, 1896, Preece, in a lecture on "Telegraphing Without Wires," said that he had faith in Marconi and his work.

Soon afterwards, Marconi was summoned back to Italy by the Ministry of War, to enroll for the three years' military training required of all Italian citizens. Faced by this setback to his scientific work, Marconi appealed to the Italian Embassy in London. He was finally assigned to the Embassy as a naval student so that he could continue his experiments.

He began by transmitting signals from a room in the London General Post Office, first to a neighboring roof, then to Salisbury Plain. Next he made tests across the Bristol Channel. In July, 1897, a company—eventually known as Marconi's Wireless Telegraph Co., Ltd.—was formed to install wireless on lightships and lighthouses along the coast.

Marconi dreamed of sending wireless messages across the Atlantic, but transmitting over such a long distance would require apparatus far more efficient than any he had. First he began to experiment with higher and better aerials and decided that ten-foot balloons covered with tinfoil would make good antennae. But the strong winds necessary to lift them also blew them to pieces, and shreds of tinfoiled balloons were soon scattered over the English countryside. Then Marconi made long-tailed kites to which tinfoil had been fastened. From these aerials it was possible to broadcast for eight or nine miles. Later, on the Isle of Wight, "Marconigrams" were sent with a one-hundred-and-twenty-foot aerial supported by a strong mast and connected to a transmitter. To test the apparatus, Marconi went to sea on a tug. Using an antenna suspended from a mast, he could hear signals over a distance of eighteen miles.

Lloyds of London was ready to install Marconi instruments in all their lighthouse posts, and Marconi stations were erected which could communicate with vessels twenty-five miles from shore. Even then Marconi thought in terms of the wireless lighthouse, the radio direction finder, and the radio beacon—all of which later proved vital to safe navigation, in the air as well as on the sea. The shipping companies also began to install wireless, and in 1900 the British Admiralty had the Marconi system set up in twenty-six warships.

Unfortunately, one great obstacle, that of interference, prevented the widespread use of wireless by individuals. If a number of stations were transmitting at the same time, the messages were jumbled together, and there was no way of sorting them out. To obviate this difficulty, Marconi developed the idea of tuning.

Sir Oliver Lodge had shown that by tuning together both transmitter and receiver, a station that was receiving on one wave length was not affected by a message of a different wave length: the aerial would respond only to the wave length for which it was tuned. Marconi adopted Lodge's suggestion, and made a series of improvements in the apparatus. He further demonstrated that it was possible to receive messages from different transmitting stations by varying the number of turns in the coil of the antenna circuit of the receiver.

Marconi's greatest triumph came in December, 1901, when he first bridged the Atlantic with wireless signals. The very next month he received signals two thousand miles from the coast of Cornwall, while on a steamship bound for New York.

To prove that wireless messages would travel as rapidly from west to east as in the opposite direction, Marconi next selected Glace Bay, Nova Scotia, as a site for his transmitter. While the station was being erected, he accepted from the Italian government a cruiser, *Carlo Alberto,* to facilitate long-distance tests of his new magnetic detector, which was like a hypersensitive mechanical ear. After further work on his equipment, he decided, in December, 1902, to see if he could reach Cornwall, England, from Nova Scotia. At that time the sending key was fully three feet long. As he pressed the key, the noise was like a machine gun, and long sparks jumped from the knobs of the huge Leyden jars. In a few minutes the return signals came, the first clear daytime message from a coast over two thousand miles away. Near his Nova Scotia station, the *La Bourgogne* had sunk five years before with nearly all her passengers. Seeing a freighter which marked the spot, Marconi said that aid could have been summoned from Newfoundland if the *La Bourgogne* had been equipped with wireless.

Wireless was demonstrated at the St. Louis World's Fair in 1904. Before long, amateurs and engineers all over the world were experimenting with the new apparatus. When its value was fully realized, various efforts were made to discredit the Marconi Company through patent infringements. The matter was fought out in the courts, and Marconi won. Judge Van Vechten Veeder, in summarizing the entire history of wireless, held that all patents filed in the United States by Guglielmo Marconi were valid. He cited evidence that Marconi was "the first to discover and use any practical means for effective telegraphic transmission and intelligible reception of signals produced by artificially formed Hertz oscillations."

Edison, who had backed Marconi in all his research, himself had applied for a patent in 1885, the drawings for which show high-pole aerials on either side of a stream, connected to a signaling apparatus consisting of a telephone receiver, a telegraph key, and batteries. Edison had refused to sell his patent to other companies, but allowed the Marconi Company to have it in exchange for a share of stock.

It took a disaster at sea to make the public realize the full value of Marconi's discovery. In April, 1912, the *S.S. Titanic* steamed toward New York with two thousand persons aboard. She had wireless apparatus of the latest design, though not of sufficient power for her to remain in communication with shore unless messages were relayed by other vessels. Although the weather was clear, icebergs were reported not many miles from the shipping lane she was following. Nevertheless, the *Titanic* plunged ahead at the rate of nearly twenty-five miles an hour.

It was nearly midnight, and the *Titanic* was 1,284 miles east of Sandy Hook, New Jersey, when lookouts suddenly reported a large iceberg directly ahead. But the *Titanic* was going too fast. The ship crashed, and the giant iceberg ripped her open beneath the water line for three hundred feet.

The *Titanic,* fated to sink within three hours, lay six hundred miles off Cape Race. The ship began a forward list. Rockets went up, red lights flared, and John G. Phillips, the senior wireless operator, sent frantic signals giving latitude and longitude.

The wireless had weakened, and the engine rooms had flooded, when responses came. The *Carpathia* had picked up the signal, but she was so far away that it took her until morning to reach the ship in distress. Meanwhile, Phillips signaled the SOS until all the lifeboats had been filled. Then someone strapped a lifebelt to his back and dragged him to the last raft, but Phillips was so exhausted from exposure that he died. Hundreds of passengers were in the water and other hundreds were crowded into small boats. Although other vessels steamed to the *Titanic's* aid, many passengers died in the icy water. But many others owed their lives to wireless.

In 1922 the Western Electric Company bought

some broadcasting time from the American Telephone and Telegraph Company, and sponsored a program of entertainment over station WEAF in New York. From that time on, broadcasting became a thriving business. Marconi had devised a crystal detector set (then priced at $25.50) which was greeted by the press as "Radio for Everybody." Then the vacuum tube was invented, a tremendous advance. When, in 1922, Marconi sailed to America in his yacht, the *Elettra,* which he used as a floating laboratory, he was greeted by radio music when he docked in New York Harbor, and the Institute of Radio Engineers gave him an ovation. When the *Elettra* steamed up the Hudson to Albany, he was welcomed by Steinmetz and other distinguished scientists.

Marconi's whole interest centered upon wireless telegraphy until his death in 1937. From his childhood, he had directed all his energies to it, crossing the ocean eighty-nine times for his scientific work. Despite the success of his experiments, he did not make a great deal of money, and left an estate of only $200,000 when he died—exactly the cost of his first transatlantic message.

Marconi was a shy, retiring person and was considered very difficult to meet. He also had a reputation for sincerity. But most of all, he was a man who had a good idea and stuck to it. That idea seemed so simple that Marconi often said, "It was unbelievable to me that no one had thought of it before."

CHAPTER 10

Luther Burbank

The botanist named Luther Burbank spent most of his
life in orchards, gardens, and nurseries, working close
to the soil as he bred new and better plant varieties.
Yet during his lifetime he was a controversial figure
and his scientific work was denounced in newspapers
and from pulpits.

Luther Burbank, the thirteenth of fifteen children, was born in Lancaster, Massachusetts, on March
7, 1849. He was a rather sensitive, shy boy, with an
inordinate curiosity about the out-of-doors. His cousin,
Professor Levi Burbank, took him on long walks in the
woods to study plant life, and Luther liked to read the
books of Henry Thoreau, who wrote of his life alone
in the woods and of the wild life he studied and loved.
Another influence on the boy Luther was Louis Agassiz,

the great naturalist, who was a friend of the Burbank family.

Luther Burbank completed his formal education at Lancaster Academy, where he studied biology, chemistry, and physics. But he had not yet decided upon a career. He wanted to study medicine, but there were so many children in the family and so little money that he was forced to go to work. He got a job in a near-by factory as a wood turner and pattern maker for fifty cents a day. Here he invented a machine that could do the work of six men, and his wages were increased to ten dollars a day. But he did not enjoy the work, which was all indoors, and it did not improve his rather poor health. When his father died, Luther used his small inheritance to buy a seventeen-acre farm near Lancaster, and, at the age of twenty-one, became a truck gardener.

It was at this time that Luther Burbank first read Charles Darwin's *Animals and Plants Under Domestication*. He decided then and there to make plant breeding his lifework. While he had no real scientific education, he did have intense curiosity about plants and a love of nature. He began simple experiments, and, through trial and error, improved growing methods. These he tested in further experiments, as he tried to develop new and sturdier vegetables. One of his first adventures was with sweet corn. To get his own corn on the market early, he "forced" the kernels inside the warm house two weeks before the ground was ready.

Then, when it was warm enough outside, he planted his seeds which had already sprouted. In this way he gained two weeks on the other gardeners, and his sweet corn was ready to sell two weeks earlier in the summer.

One day Burbank discovered among his potato plants a seed ball—an infrequently found cluster of seeds in the leafy part of the plant. He carefully collected and planted twenty-three seeds from the ball. Then he selected the two best plants that grew from these seeds. The next year he planted the potatoes of these two plants and they in turn produced potatoes larger, whiter, smoother, and sweeter than any yet grown. In fact, they were so superior that they were almost like a new vegetable. These potatoes, with further improvements, developed into the Burbank potato, destined to be talked about all over the world and to earn millions of dollars for farmers. In Ireland the people depended on the potato for food. Their crops had been getting smaller, and thousands of plants, diseased and inferior, were dying out every year. When this new Burbank potato was introduced, Ireland's most important food gained new life and the Irish no longer suffered from a potato shortage.

But all this was far in the future when Burbank exhibited his first new potato plants at a neighborhood fair. He sold several of them to a well-known seedsman for $150. With this money Burbank set out for California, where he could continue his work unhindered by the long winters and short growing season of Massachusetts. He was twenty-six when he came to the Santa Rosa Valley, where the climate was mild and the soil rich and varied. He had only ten dollars in his pocket when he arrived, ten potatoes in his suitcase, and the suit of clothes which he wore. But he was delighted with the California climate and the luxuriance of the vegetation. He wrote East a few days after his arrival, commenting on the lack of fog and harsh winds and enthusiastically describing a pear he had bought for five cents, a pear so big that he could eat only two-thirds of it. He was desperately poor, and for several months he took any work he could find: lathing, cleaning chicken coops, any odd job that paid him a little.

In time he got a steady job in a flower nursery where he received very small wages. To save money he slept in an attic over the greenhouse. There he became seriously ill. When he recovered he managed to scrape together enough money to buy a small plot of land and here he established a nursery. He was now twenty-eight. In his first year as "the nurseryman south of the Iron Bridge" in Santa Rosa he made a profit of $15.20.

Burbank's first big order was from a man named Warren Dutton, who, when he heard that the new dried-prune industry was profitable, had bought some orchard land with the idea of going into business. In the early spring of 1881, he came to Luther Burbank, who had been in Santa Rosa for several years. Dutton wanted twenty thousand prune trees delivered to him for planting in December. The order seemed almost impossible to fill, for prune trees grow slowly. A prune seed planted in March could not be expected to produce a tree suitable for transplanting to an orchard in December. Burbank considered the proposition overnight and then said that he would take the order if Dutton would finance the project. Dutton agreed, and Burbank immediately set to work. He prepared special beds, bought thirty thousand almond stones and planted them. Almonds sprout quickly and are rapid growers, and in a very short time the stones had put forth sprouts and begun to grow. At the end of June, Burbank bought prune buds from a neighbor's healthy orchard and for two months he and his crew budded the prune buds into the almond seedlings. By December the young prune trees were ready and Dutton received his order on time.

News soon spread about the young nurseryman who was getting such startling results from plant breeding. He began to receive inquiries from near and far and built up a good seed business. But Burbank was always primarily interested in his search for new and improved plant varieties. In his work he would cross one variety with another, then choose the sturdiest, healthiest specimens from the resulting hybrids, destroying all those that did not come up to standard—and then the process would be repeated, and repeated again. He might be looking for a fruit that was a heavy bearer, or one with a certain color, or one that would stand shipping or be particularly good for canning. So

he would select and reselect through several generations until he found the perfect fruit with the special
qualities he was seeking. He would walk through the
beds and tie a piece of white cloth on the plants he
chose for further experiment. The chosen few would
be tended, watched, and the best of them—sometimes
just one or two which had the exact quality required
—selected for breeding.

Burbank was earning a good income from the sale
of seeds and trees, but he found that business took too
much time from his scientific work, so he gave up his
nursery and bought four acres of land near his first
plot. With his mother and a sister, who had come from
Massachusetts to live with him, he moved into a cottage
on the property and began to prepare his land for the
work he was to pursue for the rest of his life. To this
acreage he later added a farm of sixteen acres at Sebastopol, California. He found that by planting many
seeds for one project—sometimes ten thousand of one
kind—he would have a wide selection and his results
would be better. He wrote some of the seed companies
in England, the Continent, the Orient, and Australia,
describing his California seeds and offering them for
sale.

Burbank was enthusiastic about his work. He
loved to take walks in the California hills looking for
unusual plants and collecting seeds. If he saw a particularly interesting wild flower in the spring, he would
mark it with a piece of cloth and come back in the fall

to gather its seeds. Sometimes he ran out of cloth and was forced to tear up his handkerchief or his necktie or perhaps use a shoestring. More than once he came flopping home with both shoelaces gone, excited by some unusual discovery.

As people began to hear more about the young plant breeder, letters and seeds came pouring in from all over the world. In one letter from New Guinea were rock melon and cantaloupe seeds that would stand excessive moisture, and the writer promised to send seeds from a strange plum. A woman wrote him about some squash, bean, and corn seeds that explorers had taken from the ruins of the cliff dwellers in the Grand Canyon. Some corn kernels arrived from the grave of a Zulu king in Africa. When Burbank crossed California flowers and fruits with the seeds and plants he received from distant places, he obtained interesting new strains.

One of these was the plum. At that time the plum was tiny, large-stoned, usually sour, and almost impossible to ship. In a sailor's description of his voyages, Burbank had read of a "blood-red" plum that grew in Japan, so in 1885 he sent to a Japanese dealer in Yokohama for twelve plum seedlings of various types. These little trees were sturdy and thrived in the California soil. Their fruit was large, bright in color, and small-stoned, but it had its faults, too. Some of the plums lacked flavor, some were almost juiceless; some bloomed so early that they were caught by late frost or spring rains. Burbank crossed the Japanese plum with American and European varieties. The resulting hybrid was not much better than either parent. But after several generations and thousands of crossings, improvements could be seen. From these thousands about on hundred satisfactory trees resulted, from which were developed six superior plum varieties. The Wickson was the best of all. Its tree has a pleasing shape, the fruit is abundant, large, with firm, delicious flesh, and the stone is small and does not cling. If this plum is picked when ripe, it can be kept for two weeks; if it is picked before it is ripe and then shipped, it will still ripen and retain its flavor.

In 1893, Burbank published a catalogue with the title, *New Creations in Fruits and Flowers*. Here he listed about one hundred new plants, flowers, berries, and trees that he had produced by scientific combinations. There was a new walnut that grew much more rapidly and produced nuts sooner than other walnut trees; there were four new varieties of quince, ten new plums and prunes, many improved berries, a long list of vegetables, and new flowers, including the first double gladiolus and a silver poppy.

Publication of the catalogue caused a storm of protest. Those who believed that heredity alone influenced life were furious because Burbank at the end of the catalogue had summed up his theory of plant development and stated that plant life was strongly influenced and changed by its environment. Many nurserymen were angry or disbelieving. Critics charged him with blasphemy, for he had claimed to bring forth "new creations," and they thought no man could or should have the power of creation. He received bitter letters; he was called all kinds of names; ministers preached against him in the churches. But nurserymen bought his stock, and inside of a year almost all of the plants listed in the catalogue had been sold. Burbank was called "The Plant Wizard" but he insisted that he had no magic qualities. What Burbank did have was great curiosity, knowledge of plants, a special gift for selection, and capacity for hard work.

In 1905 the Carnegie Institute acknowledged the importance of Burbank's experiments by granting him $10,000 a year for his work in plant development. At the same time the Institute sent several of its research experts to study his methods. Burbank had thought the grant would free him from financial worry and allow him to devote all his time to experiments. But unfortunately the research experts, who wanted to record every detail of Burbank's work, took so much of his time that he could not continue the arrangement.

Among the most curious of Burbank's experiments —to plant breeders it was almost unbelievable—was the one he did with cactus. He wanted to remove the spines from this plant and make it productive so that the desert area of the American Southwest might have a profitable crop. Over a period of sixteen years he experimented with various cacti collected and shipped to him from the southwestern states and Mexico. The cactus, he believed, had borne edible fruit many years ago, and he hoped to bring this about again. He succeeded in producing a cactus which, growing with little trouble in the desert, would produce one hundred and fifty to three hundred tons of fodder per acre. One acre of five-year plants would produce fifty to one hundred tons of fruit. This cactus multiplied rapidly by division, and was unusually hardy. Cactus experimentation is still going on, but Burbank was a pioneer in the field.

Many of Burbank's experiments were doomed to failure. For example, he tried without success to cross the tomato and potato. He did produce a vegetable from the union, but not one that could be grown to commercial advantage.

At Burbank's Sebastopol farm a single acre grew several thousand different varieties of fruit. This Burbank accomplished by grafting onto one tree many different varieties—sometimes as many as one hundred on a single apple tree. This not only saved space but speeded up his experiments. Instead of waiting four to fifteen years for a young apple tree to bear, he would graft a twig from a seedling to a mature bearing tree. In two or three years this new branch would produce fruit. He developed an improved cherry, a thornless blackberry, a larger, sweeter raspberry almost free of prickles. He delighted flower lovers with his Shasta daisy, and the fragrant rose, later given his name. Many medals and prizes were awarded to him for his products.

Burbank did not marry until he was sixty-seven. By then he had become very well known throughout the world. His mail was tremendous, and his acquaintances included many famous people. Jack London was his neighbor; John Burroughs was a favorite friend; he knew Henry Ford and Thomas Edison; Paderewski visited him a number of times; the great singer Mme. Schumann-Heink was his guest. The great and the near-great flocked to his farm to see him, for everyone enjoyed meeting this stooped little man with the sly sense of humor, who was as extravagant in his everyday speech as he was exact in his work and in the reports of his experiments.

Toward the end of his life, Burbank found time to write or dictate a great deal about his methods and results. He also gave lectures on his work occasionally, although he did not enjoy speaking in public. In March, 1926, in a San Francisco church, he denounced the false teaching and superstition that clouded the truths he had discovered in nature and science. A schoolteacher in the South had been brought to trial for teaching Darwin's theory of evolution, and Burbank felt that his words in support of Darwin's theory and in condemnation of narrow religious beliefs would carry some weight. A tremendous controversy followed this public address, and he was flooded with letters and telegrams of protest as well as congratulations for his courage. He felt that he should answer all these letters, and the strain of this extra work, plus his reaction to the abuse heaped upon him, were too much for his health, which had never been good. He desperately wanted to make people understand the truth of his statements. But he was an old man. The effort proved too much for him, and he fell ill and died. At his own request, he was buried beneath a cedar near his home, a cedar he loved and had planted himself.

CHAPTER 11

Walter Reed

If Walter Reed had been able to grow a beard—the badge of his profession—he might have lived and died a country doctor. But he was under twenty-one. He had no whiskers, and the people in his home town refused to take him seriously. In those days a physician without a sleek Vandyke was almost worse than none at all.

The smooth-faced young man was discouraged. Here he was with his new degree in medicine, and he could not make a living. Even worse, he could not do what he had always planned, curb and comfort human suffering.

There was only one thing left for Walter Reed to do. Sadly, he packed his bags and said goodbye to his mother and father, who was a Methodist minister.

Then he left his home in the little settlement of Belroi, Virginia, where he had been born on September 13, 1851.

Walter Reed went to the city of New York, where he took another medical degree at Bellevue Medical College (he had received his first from the University of Virginia when he was only seventeen). Then he served as a house surgeon in the Brooklyn City Hospital and in the City Hospital on Blackwell's Island, and as a New York City district physician. He was appointed one of five inspectors of the Brooklyn Board of Health—at the age of twenty-two!

In 1875, the brilliant young physician entered the Medical Corps of the United States Army. For eighteen years he was medical officer at various army posts throughout the country. He spent four years in Arizona; five in the Department of the Platte; two in the Department of Dakota; three in the South; and three years in the East.

His early practice in the Far West, where doctors were few in those days, gave the studious Lieutenant Reed experience that proved of great help to him in later years. For to the isolated outposts where he was stationed, settlers came for treatment of their ills. As he cared for these people, he learned how to face emergencies of all kinds.

Then, with this practical training behind him, Dr. Reed began what was to be his real career. He was assigned to duty as an attending surgeon in Baltimore.

It was a stroke of fortune that started him out on the road to future greatness.

For to the serious young doctor, Baltimore meant Johns Hopkins Medical School. And Johns Hopkins meant, most importantly, Professor William Welch. Walter Reed took advantage of a wonderful opportunity. He registered for special studies in bacteriology and pathology under the world-famed professor.

By 1898, Dr. Reed—then Major—occupied a firm position in the scientific world. Besides his duties as a medical officer, he was curator of the Army Medical Museum in Washington, and Professor of Bacteriology in the newly organized Army Medical School.

At the outbreak of the Spanish-American War, Major Reed was chosen to head the fight against typhoid fever, a dread disease in army camps. His investigations—they took more than a year and required remarkable skill and patience—proved the importance of the common fly as a carrier of infection and showed how typhoid spread from man to man by contact, or through infected bedding, tents, and implements. This information was immediately put to use by the Army to control typhoid epidemics.

Reed's successful battle with typhoid fever, however, was little more than a warm-up for the championship fight of his career. Before much time had passed, typhoid was not the menace it once had been. But the United States' volunteer armies were threatened by something worse—yellow fever.

Few people today realize how awful was the fear of "yellow jack." The disease had preyed over the length and breadth of the New World. In Haiti it had destroyed one of Napoleon's expeditionary forces. It had killed one hundred thousand Americans before the Republic was fairly established. Florida, Texas, and Louisiana were dangerous places to live during certain months of the year. States along the Mississippi River were forced to maintain "shotgun quarantines" to keep out suspects from yellow-fever zones. Yellow jack had even come as far north as New York, and in panic, people fled from the city. In only thirty days, one-tenth of Philadelphia's population was killed by yellow fever.

Now, in 1900, this plague was attacking the American soldiers who were in Havana to set up the Cuban Republic. Already more soldiers had been killed by the yellow jack than by the bullets of the Spanish enemy. And it wasn't like most diseases, which breed in dirt and poverty. Yellow jack killed the clean and the dirty, the rich and poor, soldiers and civilians. More than one-third of the commanding general's staff themselves were victims.

The general, Leonard Wood, issued orders to improve sanitary conditions. Still the disease raged to plague proportions. He commanded Havana to be scrubbed. Yellow fever climbed to its highest peak in twenty years. Then, in desperation, General Wood sent out a call for Walter Reed, in Washington.

Major Reed was well equipped for the assignment. He had been in pestholes before. He had grown up in the Civil War, and neither war nor pestilence could dismay him. Then, too, he had already had some experience with yellow fever. Only recently he had overthrown the claim of Sanarelli, a distinguished bacteriologist who insisted he had discovered the organism that caused yellow fever.

On June 25, 1900, in the heat of a Cuban summer, Walter Reed arrived from Washington. The epidemic now was at its worst. He found the hospital at Quemados full of yellow fever cases. Young American soldiers were dying every day, and many more were desperately ill.

Three men, with Reed, were to make up the "Yellow Fever Commission." Dr. James Carroll had come with him from Washington. Already in Cuba were a European-trained bacteriologist, Jesse Lazear, and Aristides Agramonte, a Cuban who, unlike the others, had already had yellow fever.

But the commissioners were stopped almost before they started. In their first eighteen case studies they could not find a microbe. July was the time when yellow fever struck hardest, and there were many grave cases among the eighteen, but they were unable to isolate a single bacillus.

Walter Reed, however, was too old a hand at microbe hunting to let this failure stop him. He was determined to investigate every possibility—take every chance if need be—that might put him on the road to victory.

It was then that Walter Reed remembered Dr. Carlos Finlay's theory. Dr. Finlay was a physician in Havana, a man who was not taken seriously even by his friends; for he had a strange "hallucination." He had no reasons for it, but he stuck to his belief.

"Yellow fever," he insisted, "is caused by a mosquito!"

Walter Reed, grasping at straws, decided to take a chance. But again he was stopped almost before he started. He had the mosquitoes—but on what could he experiment? He knew already that not even monkeys or apes could be used as experimental animals. They would not contract yellow fever. There was but one solution: He must risk human lives.

But where would he get the men?

Now the members of the commission showed their stature. Quickly they agreed: They would be the guinea pigs themselves. They would not subject other lives to danger. James Carroll and Jesse Lazear were the first to volunteer.

The experiments had scarcely begun when Major Reed was called away on official business. When he returned from Washington, he found that tragedy had felled his men. Lazear was dead, of the bite of infected mosquitoes. Carroll, not far from death, was only now recovering.

The time had come for decision. One man was already dead. Should the experiment continue?

Walter Reed looked at the rows of men dying in hospital wards—and decided that the research must go on. First he offered himself as a guinea pig, but his associates opposed him. How could the project continue if their leader himself should die? His self-sacrifice defeated, Reed went to General Leonard Wood, who was increasingly worried about the threat of yellow fever to his men. Wood backed him to the limit, giving him money to build a camp of seven tents and two little houses about a mile from Quemados.

His isolation ward completed—it was named Camp Lazear to honor the man who had given his life for others—Walter Reed began a series of airtight tests. When he called for volunteers, two men stepped forward. They faced near certain death, for eighty-five of every one hundred men with yellow fever were dying; and the most they could hope for was a small government pension as reward.

The two men, Private Kissenger and John J. Moran, a civilian, thought for a moment. Then they made a simultaneous announcement. They would agree to the tests all right—but on one important condition: They would expose themselves to danger only if they were *not* paid for it.

The two men then went into quarantine, where they allowed themselves to be stung by mosquitoes that had bitten human beings in the last stages of yellow fever. Kissenger, bitten by two mosquitoes that had fed on the blood of dying soldiers, was the first victim. He fell ill with yellow fever, and lived to tell about it. Then Moran caught it, and he too lived.

These were the first in a series of cases. When Major Reed had completed this stage of his project, he had proved conclusively that yellow fever *is* caused by the bite of a mosquito.

Dr. Reed was elated. He wrote to his wife: "Rejoice with me, sweetheart, as aside from the antitoxin of diphtheria and Koch's discovery of the tubercle bacillus, it will be regarded as the most important piece of work, scientifically, during the nineteenth century."

Victory was now in sight. But Major Reed was a thorough scientist who believed in testing every possibility. Even the old theories of contagion and contamination must be tried. Through long nights of horror, his volunteers lay in the blankets and the clothing of other men who had died of yellow fever. Reed, bearing full responsibility, sleepless and torn with anxiety, watched the experiments.

But the windows were screened, and his volunteers did not fall prey to the yellow jack. The proof was now conclusive. Contagion did not cause fever. Mosquitoes alone were responsible.

Dr. Reed wrote again to his wife: "The prayer that has been mine for twenty years, that I might be permitted in some way or at some time to do something to alleviate human suffering, has been granted!"

Walter Reed's prayer had been answered in a way he had never dreamed of as a beardless doctor in the little town that refused to take him seriously. For when the results of his work were made public, American sanitary engineers went to work. General Gorgas cleared mosquitoes from Havana so effectively that in three months not a case of yellow fever remained. The city was free of yellow jack at last, after two hundred years!

Cities and ports that had been pestholes for centuries soon were without a trace of the disease. Today it has been almost entirely eliminated throughout the world.

Walter Reed died on November 23, 1902, at the Army General Hospital in Washington, D.C. Then fifty-one, he was regarded as one of the world's most prominent bacteriologists.

Major Reed had become ill with acute appendicitis eight days before his death. He had been operated on, but never rallied from his surgery. His last words were of regret.

"I leave so little," he said.

It is true that he had little property to leave his wife and children. But to the world he left something precious—freedom from a terrible disease. On his tombstone in Arlington Cemetery are the words that Charles Eliot, President of Harvard, had said of him:

"He gave to man control over that dreadful plague, yellow fever."

The world's gratitude is not always prompt, and, like many other great men, Walter Reed did not receive full recognition in his lifetime for his services to man. In the years succeeding his death, however, some measure of tribute was paid this simple man who wanted only to serve humanity. His home in Belroi, Gloucester County, was made a national shrine; a research fund was established in his name at the University of Virginia; and a great Army hospital was named for him in Washington, D.C.

CHAPTER 12

Arthur, Karl, and Wilson Compton

One day in October, 1932, an unusual event took place at Western College, in Oxford, Ohio. There, for the first time in history, a degree was awarded, not for professional accomplishment, but for motherhood.

When Otelia Augspurger Compton, a tall, gray-haired woman of seventy-four, rose to accept her degree, the president of Western College addressed her. "You have given useful children to the nation," he said. "We want to honor you for it."

Then he conferred upon this aging woman, who once had been a country school teacher, an honorary LL.D., a Doctor of Laws degree.

Seated on the platform to see their mother honored, were three of Mrs. Compton's children: handsome men in their early forties. The presentation of degrees was no novelty to these three men; among them they held a total of forty-six. Karl, the oldest, a noted physicist, had made important discoveries about photo-electric effects and the structure of crystals. Wilson, the second son, was an administrator and an economist. Arthur, the youngest, had already won a Nobel Prize in physics.

The father of these distinguished men, Professor Elias Compton, was also in the audience. He had been a member of the faculty of Wooster College for forty-five years, twenty-two of them as dean.

Only one member of the family did not see her mother in a scholar's cap and gown. Mary could not come home. She lived in Allahabad, India, where she ran a missionary school and her husband was president of a college. Mary sent a cable to her mother, the first of many messages of congratulation Otelia Compton received.

One eighty-year-old woman, who had worked to educate her six children, wrote that she was glad "that colleges which give honors to nag-raisers and good cattle and sheep at last honor motherhood." Others who wrote to Mrs. Compton wanted to know how she had managed to rear such a distinguished family. Had she studied books on child care and psychological theories?

Mrs. Compton laughed at questions like these. "There wasn't any book to guide me," she said, "unless it was the Bible."

One of the stories Mrs. Compton told about her sons reveals something about the kind of mother she was. Once Arthur, who was then eight years old, came to her with an essay he had written. "I have gone through a lot of books," he said. "They all say that African elephants have three toes and Indian elephants five toes. I think this is wrong. I say African elephants have five toes and Indian elephants have three toes, and this," he concluded, handing her his essay, "is why I think so."

Although what her son was attempting to prove was not correct, Mrs. Compton read the essay carefully and told him that he had done well to investigate the matter so thoroughly. Thirty years later she asked him whether he remembered this incident.

Arthur smiled, said "yes," and added, "If you had laughed at me then, it would have finished my urge for research."

At a time when many parents believed that they knew exactly what was right for their children and enforced their ideas rigidly, Otelia Compton allowed her family considerable freedom. Although all her children had chores they were expected to do, these were never allowed to interfere with their hobbies and interests.

Karl, who liked to read—the *Iliad* was one of his favorite books—wrote a book on Indian fighting when he was twelve. Mary taught herself languages. Arthur's primary interest was astronomy. His parents bought a telescope for him and, although the neighbors criticized them for it, allowed their son to sit up all night studying the stars.

The four Compton children were all under ten when their mother took them on a trip to the woods of northern Michigan. There they hewed a clearing, pitched a tent, and enjoyed living for a while as pioneers. Wilson, especially, loved the woods. When he grew up, he became an expert on forestry, an interest that began on this childhood vacation.

Through high school and college, the Compton boys earned their own money and had their own bank accounts. Karl, who worked on farms and once drove a mule team, took his jobs very seriously.

In college the Comptons had excellent athletic, as well as academic, records. Each of the boys won three letters in major sports. Karl stood out most of all. Once he climbed the inside of a 140-foot smokestack to place a class banner at the top. But his crowning achievement was to break a tie in a football game with what was the longest drop-kick in Wooster College history.

The Compton boys all graduated from Wooster with Phi Beta Kappa keys; later they all received doctor's degrees from Princeton University. But after they left Wooster College, their paths led in different directions. Wilson, who had specialized in history and economics, chose to write about the lumber business for his Ph.D. thesis, because of his interest in forestry. Later he became an authority on such matters as wood products, lumber grading, and conservation of woodland.

Arthur was to become a well-known physicist. He had shown signs of scientific ability when he was still in his teens. He built gliders then, published articles on aeronautics, made an astronomical clock for his telescope, and photographed Halley's comet. When he was in college, he invented and patented a gyroscopic device for airplane control.

Arthur had decided that he was going to be a mechanical engineer when, partly because of his older brother Karl's influence, he changed his mind and began to study mathematics and physics. In 1916, he received his Ph.D. in physics from Princeton. Soon afterwards, with his new wife, an Ohio girl named Betty Charity McCloskey, he went to the University of Minnesota to teach physics, and after that worked as a research engineer for the lamp division of Westinghouse Electric and Manufacturing Company.

After a few years, Arthur discovered that he did not particularly like working for industry. He told his wife, with whom he always discussed his work and important decisions, that he wanted to return to academic life and to basic research. Then he applied for and received a research fellowship in the Cavendish Laboratory, in Cambridge, England. There he studied under J. J. Thomson, who first identified and weighed the electron, and Ernest Rutherford, who discovered the nucleus. He saw Rutherford perform experiments that revealed the structure of atoms and was profoundly impressed. Several years later Arthur Compton was also doing basic research in nuclear physics. He chose to study X-rays and, in the early 1920's, made a very important discovery: that after collisions with electrons, the wave lengths of X-rays increase. This phenomenon, which has been named the "Compton Effect," is of special significance because it supports Einstein's theory that light is composed of particles. For his accomplishment Arthur Compton (jointly with C. T. R. Wilson) was awarded the Nobel Prize in physics. He also won the Rumford Gold Medal of the American Academy of Arts and Sciences.

When her youngest son received a Nobel Prize, Otelia Compton was still living in the family home in Wooster, Ohio. "How did you feel when you learned the news about Arthur?" someone asked her.

Mrs. Compton replied that she had prayed that it would not "turn his head. And it didn't," she added, for he remained a simple, unassuming person. She was pleased, too, because Arthur was always, as she was, deeply religious, and he became a leading spokesman for those who see no conflict between science and religion.

In his view, and these are his words, "Science is the glimpse of God's purpose in nature. The very existence of the amazing world of the atom and radiation points to a purposeful creation, to the idea that there is a God and an intelligent purpose back of everything."

When Arthur Compton returned to America from England, he taught in, and then headed, the physics department of Washington University in St. Louis. Then he went on to the University of Chicago, where he eventually became head of the physics department. At Chicago he taught an early morning class, and then went to his office to work. This simple room was furnished with a gray rug, a black steel desk, and a cosmic-ray counter, which clicked away in a corner.

Like many other physicists, Arthur Compton had become very interested in cosmic rays, the high-speed nuclear particles that have enormous penetrating power and continuously rain on our planet from outer space. Where do these particles come from? Arc thcy affected by the earth's magnetic field? What happens to them when they enter our atmosphere? These were some of the questions Arthur Compton wanted answers to, and his investigations took him to the Arctic and the equator, to high mountains in Asia, Europe, and South America.

In 1930, with funds from the Carnegie Corporation, he organized a world-wide survey to collect cosmic ray data. Eight zones in different parts of the world were set up, and in each one a research team, equipped with a new electroscope Compton had invented, gathered information. From this broad range of observation it became clear how cosmic rays vary according to latitude.

While Dr. Compton was teaching at Chicago, he and Mrs. Compton lived with their two sons in a large brick house that was filled with souvenirs collected on cosmic ray trips. Here the physicist liked to spend occasional evenings playing the mandolin. He was a tall, rugged man who played a fast game of tennis and was a powerful swimmer.

During and after World War II, all three Compton brothers went to work, in various ways, for the United States government. Karl Compton had been president of the Massachusetts Institute of Technology for eighteen years when, in 1948, President Truman asked him to head the Defense Department's Research and Development Board. During the year he held the post, he helped develop some important military weapons, including jet rockets and the variable time fuse. Then for two years, he was chairman of the postwar Universal Military Training Commission. Shortly before his death, on June 22, 1954, Karl Compton, as chairman of a regional Atomic Energy Committee, had begun to study peacetime uses of atomic energy.

In 1951, Wilson Compton also went to work for the government. He had served as president of Washington State University and, before that, for twenty-six

years, he had managed the National Lumber Manufacturers Association. His new government position also
was administrative; he was in charge of the government
agency that ran "The Voice of America" radio program. When he accepted this new job, which he held
for a year, Wilson Compton said that he wanted to
make "The Voice of America" an information service,
not a means of spreading propaganda.

The third Compton brother, Arthur, held one of
the most important civilian positions of World War II.
He was in charge of the scientists who achieved the first
nuclear chain reaction and the first production of U-235
and plutonium for atomic bombs. Between 1942 and
1945, Arthur divided his time between the University
of Chicago, where physicists were building the first
atomic pile and calculating its chance of success; Oak
Ridge, Tennessee, the site of huge plants for separating
fissionable U-235 from the rest of uranium; and Hanford, Washington, where plutonium was produced.

When he made these trips, he traveled under a
different name—H. Comas—for his identity was top
secret. But although Arthur's work was now "classified," he still discussed it with his wife. He had insisted
that she be cleared as a "security risk" at the same time
he was, so that he would not have to keep secrets from
her and they could discuss freely what most concerned
him.

Arthur told this story in his book, *Atomic Quest,*

published in 1956, which relates, in personal, nontechnical terms, the ups and downs of the Manhattan Project, code name for the atomic program.

In 1945, the Army took over the management of the Manhattan Project, and Arthur Compton returned to academic life. He was chancellor of Washington University, in St. Louis, until 1953, when he resigned in order to begin a ten-year research project concerning the relation of science to human affairs.

In July 1961 he resigned from this project and returned to Washington University in St. Louis as a professor-at-large. On March 3, 1962, while delivering a series of lectures in Berkeley, California, he suffered a cerebral hemorrhage. He died nearly two weeks later, on March 15.

It has been said that, collectively, the Comptons have held more honorary degrees than any other American family. These honors testify to the versatility as well as to the ability of the three brothers. Two of them scientists, one an economist, all three brothers have been, in addition, educators, administrators, and men of public affairs. They have not stayed within the limits of any one specailty but have ventured out into new fields whenever they thought they could be useful.

CHAPTER 13

Alexander Fleming

One day in September of 1928, a small but sturdy Scotsman, in early middle age, walked into his laboratory at St. Mary's Hospital in London. His tiny room looked like an old-fashioned drugstore: test tubes, retorts, microscopes, and Bunsen burners littered the table. Walnut bookcases, filled with apparatus, lined the walls.

The studious Scot, hard-working as ever, went about his work the way he always had. His laboratory was no more cluttered than usual. Nothing at all was different. Why should anything be changed? His apparatus was just where he had left it. Even the glass dishes—there, on the table in front of the open window —had not been moved. They contained the bacteria he had been growing for his study of influenza.

Alexander Fleming went to look at them. He

picked up one dish, then put it down. He looked at another—and discarded it impatiently. He examined them all in growing annoyance. They were spoiled! The bacteria he had been growing were spoiled—strangled by a bit of green mold!

Dr. Fleming *was* annoyed. But he was too canny a Scotsman to throw his cultures away. Instead, he saved the mold, and examined it under a microscope. Around the greenish stuff—it looked like the mold on Roquefort cheese—there had formed a ring, an area perfectly free of bacteria.

That clue was enough for the alert Scotsman. He knew that here—right under his own microscope—he had found a substance that would kill bacteria. What he did not realize then was that he—Alexander Fleming— had discovered penicillin, miracle drug of the twentieth century.

Alexander Fleming, who discovered the most valuable microbe destroyer ever known, was born in 1881 at Lochfield, near Darvel, Scotland. He was the seventh of eight children born of the marriage of Hugh Fleming, a farmer in this remote Ayrshire district.

Little is known of Alexander's childhood. Like so many Scotsmen, he respected the privacy of personal life—including his own. He was, in fact, so reticent about his early years that he had but one comment to make. He lived, he said, on a farm "down at the end of the road."

A few other facts, however, have filtered through

the censorship imposed by Dr. Fleming's modesty. It is known that he went to London when he was fourteen to live with an older brother who was practicing medicine. It is also known that he attended Kilmarnock Academy. There he was such a brilliant student that he walked away with almost all the available prizes and scholarships—a practice which soon became habitual.

When it was time for professional training, young Fleming decided to go to St. Mary's Hospital Medical School. He went there, he said, because St. Mary's had a championship swimming team—and he loved to swim. What the reticent scientist did not say about his medical school career is this: Here, too, he was a brilliant student, as brilliant as he had been at Kilmarnock. He quickly won academic distinction. He received numerous class prizes, the senior entrance scholarship, and—as a student at London University—took honors in physiology, pharmacology, medicine, pathology, forensic medicine, and hygiene.

In 1906, Alexander Fleming became Dr. Fleming, bacteriologist. He received his licentiate of the Royal College of Physicians, his membership in the Royal College of Surgeons, and won the university's bacteriology professorship—all in the same year!

It was an accident, the modest Dr. Fleming said with a smile, that he became a bacteriologist. There just happened to be a vacancy in bacteriology when he graduated from St. Mary's.

During the next few years, Dr. Fleming devoted

almost all his attention to research, working under the direction of Dr. Almroth Wright, pioneer in the vaccine treatment of disease. Then the First World War took him away from St. Mary's. He went to France to specialize in war wounds as a captain in the Royal Medical Corps.

In France, the brilliant bacteriologist found a task worthy of his capabilities. The antiseptics being used to treat the terrible wounds of war, he discovered, actually *promoted* infection. They were supposed to harm bacteria. Instead, they destroyed white blood cells, chief among the body's defenses. Dr. Fleming determined then and there that some day he would find a bacteria-fighter not harmful to animal tissue.

In 1928, Alexander Fleming found what he had been looking for. The green stuff under his microscope —the mold that had ruined his cultures—was all the clue he needed.

"The appearance of that culture plate," he said, "was such that I thought it should not be neglected."

And Dr. Fleming saw that it was *not* neglected. He himself grew the mold in test tubes, found that it thrived best in meat broth, bread, and cheese. He demonstrated that his mold *did* harm bacteria. And, most important of all, he proved in experiments with mice that it did not damage white blood cells. Here, in his own laboratory, might be *the* long-sought nontoxic microbe killer!

Eagerly he experimented with his mold. But try as he would—and this Scotsman was tenacious—he could not isolate the drug itself, the substance within his mold that actually was the germ-killer. In the hope that someone else would succeed where he had failed, Dr. Fleming published the results of his work. Like all true men of science, he was eager to share his knowledge for the common good.

But in 1929, when Fleming announced his discovery, medical men were not ready to accept an antiseptic that worked within the body, one that had been obtained from a mold. And, later, the sulfa drugs captured the limelight; researchers dropped everything else to test them. They soon found, however, that the dramatic sulfas were not a wondrous cure-all. They did not work well in infected material. They were so irritating they sometimes delayed healing. Sometimes, when used internally, they even caused severe or fatal poisoning.

Before long intense interest in the sulfa drugs subsided, and researchers began to look around for other fields of experiment. It was at this time that Dr. Howard Walter Florey, Oxford University pathologist, decided to investigate the greenish stuff Dr. Fleming had given him. With Dr. Ernst Boris Chain and Mrs. Florey, who was also a physician, he set to work.

Florey knew nothing about the properties of the chemical he was looking for, a fact which made his task extremely difficult. But he took the mold—known technically as *Penicillum notatum*—and planted it in sugar solutions.

The mold thrived in Florey's test tubes. Then, one

day, he went to his incubator to look at them. Something had happened—shining golden droplets had developed on the surface of the mold!

Florey knew then that he was on the right track. He dried these golden droplets to a yellowish-brown powder, and there was the chemical he had been looking for—natural penicillin!

The yellow powder was hard to get, and some time passed before the Oxford scientist had enough for laboratory experiments. But the tests he *had* made were staggering in their implications. As little as one part of the yellow powder in 160 million would slow the growth of bacteria. This yellow powder was hundreds, even thousands, of times more potent than the sulfa drugs.

When Dr. Florey and his associates had grown enough of the precious penicillin, they decided to try it out on animals. For this purpose they used eight mice, all previously inoculated with deadly germs.

Of this, their first test on living creatures, Dr. Florey said:

"We sat up through the night injecting penicillin every three hours into the treated group (four mice). I must confess that it was one of the more exciting moments when we found that all the untreated mice were dead and all the penicillin-treated ones alive!"

During that historic night—in an experiment rivaling Pasteur's work with sheep—Dr. Florey had turned Alexander Fleming's vision into medical reality.

Success with animals, however, did not mean that penicillin was safe for human beings. Because the new drug might prove too dangerous to use, Dr. Florey could only try it in cases obviously doomed.

His first human guinea pig was a policeman dying of a blood infection. After five days on penicillin, he said he "felt much improved." But the precious drug was so rare the supply ran out. Bacteria again multiplied and the policeman died.

Florey's second case died the same way, but others were luckier:

A seven-year-old girl was dying with gas gangrene infection. She had already lost her left arm up to her shoulder. Penicillin saved her life.

A man lay dying of a bone infection, all hope for his recovery abandoned. He, too, was saved by injections of this miraculous drug.

Case after case testified to penicillin's life-saving qualities. By 1940 its fame as a wonder medicine had spread throughout the world. Results had been astounding. Patients suffering from a variety of infections recovered rapidly. Poisonous reactions were rare. And the drug was so mild it could be applied directly to wounds.

Even Dr. Fleming, a man not given to exaggeration, was moved to speech.

"People have called it a miracle," he said. "For once in my life as a scientist, I agree. It *is* a miracle, and it will save thousands of lives."

Penicillin, however, still was not available for the

thousands who needed it. It was difficult to produce, and what little there was was needed for the Allied armies. For Alexander Fleming's penicillin had proved itself in World War II. First used in Tunisia and Sicily, it saved the lives of countless soldiers who otherwise would have died of infection.

By 1945, penicillin was in mass production. It was still difficult, as well as expensive, to manufacture. Nearly 160 quarts of the mold culture yielded only 100 standard doses of the drug, and it cost almost $18,000 a pound to produce. But, more important than the expense, penicillin was now on hand for everyone who needed it, soldier or civilian. Although the drug was by no means effective in every case, penicillin cures mounted into the thousands.

In June of 1944, Alexander Fleming and Howard Walter Florey were knighted by their king—Fleming for having discovered penicillin, Florey for having developed it into a drug of marvelous effect.

Other honors, too, were heaped upon them. They both received the Award of Distinction from the American Pharmaceutical Manufacturers Association. Sir Alexander was awarded the Moxon Medal by the Royal College of Physicians. And he was praised by Pope Pius, in a twenty-minute audience, as "a great benefactor of mankind."

In 1945, science crowned Sir Alexander Fleming, Dr. Chain, and Sir Howard Florey, with its highest award. The Nobel Prize for physiology and medicine was theirs, the $30,000 award to be shared equally among them.

Sir Alexander went to Stockholm to receive his award from the hands of Gustav, King of Sweden. During the ceremonies, the modest Scotsman frequently made use of a large handkerchief. He was not used to being acclaimed a scientist in the Lister tradition. Then, too, he had a cold, a bad one. He used his handkerchief so often that one spectator remarked: "Penicillin *can't* be much good for colds!"

Knighthood and the Nobel Prize did not change the simple Scotsman. Honors did not inflate his modest ego—nor did they make him talkative. He remained a shy, soft-spoken scientist, who guarded his personal life the way he always had.

Americans had the privilege of seeing the silent scientist in 1945. He came to the United States on a seven-week tour of hospitals and laboratories, "to see what you have been doing with penicillin and to pick up what information about it I can, as well as to tell the little I know about it."

Reporters dogged his every footstep, but they learned little about Alexander Fleming. They *saw* him all right, and they described him. He was a small man in his early sixties, blue-eyed and ruddy-faced. He was broad-shouldered and muscular, and he wore glasses. And, though forty-nine years had passed since he left his farm "at the end of the road" in Ayrshire, he was "Scotch as a scone" in accent and in manner.

That was about all the information anyone could get. His press interviews were brief, they were witty—and they were noncommittal.

Once, surprised that he had been recognized, he said to a reporter, "What *do* you want of me?"

"Well, sir, for example," asked the reporter, "has the discovery of penicillin ruined your life?"

Sir Alexander took a long time to answer. He appeared to be working out a number of complicated equations in his head. At long last, he said in a hoarse whisper, "Nearly."

Other reporters did manage to dig up some information about Dr. Fleming. He was, they found, married to Sara McElroy, an Irishwoman. This looked like a promising lead, so they asked him about her.

The famed bacteriologist thought for a time. Then finally he answered. "She doesn't like her first name," he said. "She works. Keeps the house. Never has a day off."

That was the end of the interview.

During his stay in the United States, Sir Alexander was honored by several American institutions. He received Doctor of Science degrees from Princeton University and the University of Pennsylvania. He was awarded the 1944 Humanitarian Award of the Variety Clubs of America. President Truman hailed him as a scientist to whom "the world owes a debt of gratitude difficult to estimate."

The fifteen American manufacturers of penicillin

—during the war they had made most of the world's supply—honored Dr. Fleming with a testimonial dinner before he left the United States. It was then that they announced establishment of an $84,000 Alexander Fleming Fund. Moneys from this fund were to be used for research at St. Mary's Hospital in London, under the direction of the great scientist himself. A more fitting tribute could not have been tendered the gentle Scot. St. Mary's meant much to him, for he spent most of his life there.

In 1949 Dr. Fleming's wife, to whom he had been married for thirty-four years, became seriously ill. He nursed her until her death. Then he began to work harder than ever and kept the door to his laboratory closed, which was unusual. His friends worried about him as he grieved, silently.

Gradually, as Dr. Fleming grew more and more interested in his research, he began to talk to his co-workers about it. One of these was a handsome, young Greek woman, Dr. Amalia Voureka, who had been working with Fleming for three years and had become his good friend. Now she often accompanied him to dinners and receptions and, when she returned to Greece to become head of a laboratory, Dr. Fleming's friends noticed his gloom. Before long, he followed her to Athens and, in 1953, Dr. Voureka and Dr. Fleming were married.

Alexander Fleming once had said that until his life became dull he would not grow old. And after his marriage, although he was in his seventies, he seemed younger and happier than ever before. The two bacteriologists worked, traveled, and played croquet together.

The Flemings had planned to return to Greece for a visit in the spring of 1955 but, without any warning, Dr. Fleming became sick and weak. He had had a heart attack but, characteristically, did not think there was any need to bother a doctor for his sake. A few hours later he died.

Some months later Lady Fleming asked André Maurois, a well-known French author, to write a book about her late husband's life. Maurois agreed and in 1959 *The Life of Sir Alexander Fleming* was published, which describes the scientist's career in colorful detail and contains reproductions of some of his paintings— done not with paint but with bacteria, which develop colors as they grow.

Penicillin manufacture is now a big business, but Dr. Fleming himself got nothing out of it. Like Banting, who discovered insulin, he took no patents—and he received no money for his discovery.

But money was not important to this scientist. He was not a machine-age specialist, cold and impersonal. He looked at research from the human standpoint. If he eased suffering, that was enough reward.

Sir Alexander, like so many of the truly great, deprecated his own accomplishments.

"Had my lab been as up-to-date as those I have

visited," he said modestly, "it is possible that I would never have run across penicillin."

Alexander Fleming may have stumbled on his life-saving chemical by chance, but like all great men of science he had the genius to make the most of what others might never have investigated.

CHAPTER 14

Albert Einstein

The special theory of relativity was published in a scientific journal at the turn of the century. Since that time the theoretical physicist, Albert Einstein, has become as well-known as generals and great political leaders. In one way, this is not surprising, because his theory caused a revolution. But it was a revolution in thought only, and few thinkers, no matter how influential, have become so famous during their own lifetimes.

When Hitler came to power in 1933, Einstein was already a symbol to the German people. They thought of him as a great German who, in upsetting the ideas of other scientists, had shown the superiority of German science.

Einstein, although neither he nor his parents observed religious customs, was also a Jew. Therefore the

Nazis would not allow him to be admired. They burned his books in public and spoke against his work in halls packed with thousands. They wrote angry, vituperative editorials about him in their newspapers.

Einstein's fame preceded him to the United States. When he came to America to live, his boat was met by reporters. From that time on Einstein was considered to be "good copy." There were few people who did not know that he had wild white hair; wore turtleneck sweaters, but no socks; and played the violin. He was thought of as a genius so great that he could not be understood by the public; as a man so eccentric that he had nothing in common with the public.

Those who knew Einstein were both amused and horrified by his reputation. He had first become famous as a German; yet he abhorred nationalism. As a Jew, he had been persecuted, yet he did not practice the Jewish religion, or any other. His religion was a private one and it had no name. He was denounced as an atheist, yet he believed in a God "who reveals himself in the harmony of all being."

Einstein's friends knew, of course, that he *was* a genius and that he had eccentricities, such as complete indifference to what he wore. But they also knew that he was gentle and friendly. One of his closest friends, a physicist named Leopold Infeld, wrote, in *Albert Einstein,* that if you could meet and talk to Einstein, without knowing that he *was* Einstein, you would still be impressed by his brilliant eyes, sense of humor, and by the fact that "whatever he might say would be the product of his own mind uninfluenced by the shrieks of the outside world."

Einstein was always a peaceful person. Even when he was a child he hated war and the regimentation that went with it. When he saw parades of soldiers, he felt that he never wanted to be one of those "poor people" who followed the leader. His parents worried about him when he was slow learning to talk, failed to play with other boys, and did poorly in school.

Albert Einstein was born in Ulm, in Southern Germany, on March 14, 1879. When he was one year old, his parents moved to the city of Munich, where his father, Hermann Einstein, went into business. Because there was no Jewish school near-by, Einstein's parents sent him to a Catholic elementary school. There he learned quite a bit about the Catholic religion but did not do well in his other subjects, particularly languages, which he found difficult. He disliked the strict discipline of school and did not want to memorize material so that later, at the teacher's order, it could be mechanically repeated. He was shy and a bit hostile. At both the elementary and secondary schools he attended, his teachers thought him stupid.

When Einstein was twelve, he read a geometry textbook and it made a deep impression on him. Many years later, in his autobiography, he referred to this textbook as a "holy booklet" because of the wonder he felt when he saw that it was possible "to get certain knowledge of the objects of experience by means of pure thinking." Einstein went on to say, in the autobiography, that this wonder was founded on an error, but it was nevertheless an experience he would always remember.

As a boy, he continued to read books about mathematics and taught himself differential and integral calculus. He also read, "with breathless attention," a six-volume work that summarized scientific discoveries up to that time. He was sure, by the time he was fifteen, that he wanted to specialize in mathematics and physics.

It was at about this time that Hermann Einstein's business failed. Bankrupt, he decided to leave Germany and start over again in Italy. Albert was left behind in Munich to finish school. He was miserable. School was bad enough; being left alone was worse. He was going to ask a doctor to certify that he was suffering from nervous exhaustion and had to have a six-month vacation in Italy, when the school solved his problem by asking him to leave, because his indifference to schoolwork set a bad example for the other students. Then Albert joined his family in Milan.

He loved Italy—the art, the music, the relaxed atmosphere. He had never felt at home in Germany; now he decided to give up his German citizenship. During this six-month vacation, he also decided that, since his father was not making enough to support him, he would become a teacher and earn his own living. It was the occupation least likely to interfere with what he wanted to do—continue his own study of mathematics and physics. To be left alone, to have time for his own work, which could only be done alone—all his life this is what mattered most to Einstein.

To prepare himself to teach, he applied for admission to the Federal Institute of Technology, in Zurich, Switzerland. He failed the entrance examination. Although he scored high in mathematics, his knowledge of botany, zoology, and languages was inadequate. Now he had to go back to secondary school, and he chose one in Switzerland. After a year, he reapplied for admission to the Institute of Technology and this time passed the examination.

Einstein's academic record was not brilliant at the Institute either. He did the required work, but most of his energy and attention was given to his own studies. This independence cost him a much-needed job at the Institute when he graduated.

While Albert was studying in Zurich, he met Mileva Marec, a fellow-student who came from Hungary and who was also very interested in physics. Albert and Mileva were married in 1901 (they later had two sons) and during the same year Albert became a Swiss citizen.

For two years after he graduated from the Institute, Einstein alternated between unemployment and temporary teaching jobs. He managed to eke out a living until, through the influence of friends, he got a steady job with a regular income. Most important, the job did not interfere much with his own work. As a patent examiner in the Swiss federal office, he found time between patents to work, secretly, on his theories. In 1905, when he was twenty-six years old, he published his special theory of relativity.

Einstein's thirty-page paper was written in a simple style, had few footnotes, and no references at all to other authorities. Its title was "On the Electrodynamics of Moving Bodies," which some physicists think is a more significant title than "The Special Theory of Relativity," as it has come to be called. In this paper, Einstein showed that there is no fixed, or absolute, standard of comparison in the universe for judging the motion of the earth or other moving systems. The only movement that can be detected and measured is relative movement: the change of position of one body in respect to another.

At the conclusion of his paper, Einstein said it followed from his theory that mass and energy are interchangeable, that mass represents stores of energy, and that energy contains a small mass. He wrote a formula for the rate of exchange between mass and energy:

$$E = mc^2$$

(in which $E =$ energy, $m =$ mass, and $c =$ speed of light). Thus Einstein revealed the reservoir of energy within the atom, and how to calculate the amount of it, thirty-four years before atoms were split.

A number of books have been written to explain

Einstein's revolutionary theory in terms that are easier to understand. Among them are Lincoln Barnett's *The Universe and Dr. Einstein* and Leopold Infeld's *Albert Einstein: His Work and Its Influence on Our World.*

In the same year that Einstein published his special relativity theory he published four other papers of great importance. One of them contained the theory of light quanta, called today the "photon theory," which showed that light, under certain circumstances, exists as packets of radiant energy. This was a milestone in the development of the quantum theory. Physics today is based on two great theories—relativity and quantum. In a single year, Einstein founded one of these theories, relativity, and made a profoundly important contribution to the other, quantum.

The first public recognition of Einstein's work came three years later, when he was asked to lecture on relativity before a group of scientists in Salzburg. Then the University of Zurich made him an associate professor.

That was in 1909 and Einstein was thirty years old. He said later that up to this time he had never known a "real physicist." Now he became a part of the world of professors and remained so for the rest of his life. He was never very comfortable in this world, because he disliked the required social calls on colleagues, the endless scholarly meetings, the academic gossip. But it was a world where, for the most part, he was left alone and could do his work in peace. In 1911, now a full professor, he taught in Prague, at the German University; then returned for a while to Zurich to join the faculty of the Institute of Technology, where he had once studied.

In 1913, on the eve of the First World War, he was asked to become a member of the renowned Prussian Academy of Science. Einstein didn't like the idea of returning to Germany, but the offer was an exceptionally good one. As director of the new Kaiser Wilhelm Physical Institute, in Berlin, he would have no official duties, few teaching obligations, and unlimited time to himself. He could not refuse. His wife, Mileva, did not want to go to Germany. Their marriage had not been a success; now they agreed to separate and later they were divorced.

In Germany, Einstein used his newly acquired leisure to complete the general theory of relativity, which involved a unified theory of gravitation. For the rest of his life he tried to extend this theory to include electromagnetic forces but was not, as far as is known today, successful. Had he achieved his goal he would have unified, in a single theory, the laws that govern all the forces known to exist in nature.

It is impossible to exaggerate the fame of Albert Einstein during the seventeen years that he lived in Germany. He was acclaimed by the public and by scientists alike. When World War I came, and Einstein was one of the very few prominent Germans who opposed it, his popularity still did not dim. He received countless honorary degrees and was appointed to innumerable learned societies. In 1922 he won the Nobel Prize in physics, and a few years later the Copley Medal of the English Royal Society. Prussia made him an honorary citizen; Potsdam erected an Einstein Tower. On his fiftieth birthday, he had to leave Berlin in order to avoid a huge celebration in his honor. Congratulatory messages filled his wastepaper baskets; the gifts would have filled a freight car.

But in the 1930's, as the Nazis grew more and more powerful, everything changed. Now, when his theory of relativity was attacked on the basis of its author's religion, Einstein became truly aware of the fact that he was a Jew. He was in the United States on a trip when Hitler became head of the German government. Einstein did not return to Germany and resigned from the Prussian Academy. The Nazis confiscated his property.

Einstein was living in England when he received an attractive invitation from the Institute for Advanced Study, in Princeton, New Jersey. They offered him a position for life—a professorship that required no teaching whatsoever—and he could name his own salary.

Einstein accepted the invitation but named a salary so low that the Institute had to raise it before he started, to keep up its own standards.

When he arrived in the United States, Einstein said, "As long as I have any choice, I will stay only in a country where political liberty, toleration, and equality of all citizens before the law is the rule." In 1940 he became a United States citizen.

Einstein's second wife, Elsa, had come with him to America. They settled down in a small house in Princeton and Einstein went on with his work.

He seldom deviated from his daily schedule. At eight o'clock in the morning he got up and, before nine, left his modest frame house, located on a narrow street shaded by tall oak and elm trees. He walked for a mile and a half, through the campus of Princeton University and along a winding country road, to the Institute for Advanced Study. Rain or shine, snow or hail, he walked to his office, and whatever the weather, he was never seen wearing hat or rubbers, or carrying an umbrella.

When he reached the Institute for Advanced Study, he went to his office on the second floor. He had been assigned a spacious two-room suite. One of the rooms was small, intended for an assistant; the other, officially the professor's room, was large and furnished with comfortable chairs, bookshelves, a big desk, and blackboard. Einstein preferred to use the smaller room —it was less cold and formal. There he would sit, with a pad on his knees, and fill sheet after sheet with equations.

Einstein was still searching for a unified field theory, a system of mathematical laws by which all the forces of the universe are governed. Unlike many contemporary physicists, he believed that it *was* possible to discover a theory or system to account for all observed facts. He once said, "The most incomprehensible thing about the world is that it is comprehensible."

Einstein worked, pad on knee, with patience and concentration. "I think and think for months, for years," he said. "Ninety-nine times the conclusion is false. The hundredth time I am right."

Shortly after noon, Einstein would leave his office and walk back home, his mind still on his work. He was not aware that the people he passed on the streets of Princeton were giving him curious stares. He stood out: the great physicist, his long wavy hair glistening silver-white in the sun, his deep-set brilliant eyes; and, of course, his clothes—baggy pants, a light-blue turtle-neck sweater or an old brown leather jacket, and if you looked closely, no socks. The carelessness, even primitiveness, of Einstein's dress had a purpose. He deliberately spent as little time as he could on the things he considered least important so that he would have more time for the essential thing, his work.

Although Einstein's thoughts were faraway as he walked to his home, and though he looked inapproachable, some brave people would go up and speak to him. For them, Einstein always had a beaming smile. There was a story told around Princeton that one twelve-year-old girl went to see Einstein every day on her way home from school.

"What on earth do you talk about every afternoon?" the girl's mother asked Einstein when she found out.

He laughed and said, "She brings me cookies and I do her arithmetic homework for her."

When he reached home and had had lunch, Einstein went back to work, in his small study. Here, too, he used only a pad and pencil, filling sheet after sheet with numbers and symbols. When he rose to pace the room in thought, he would sometimes drop papers on the floor or on one of the tables that were already littered with books, letters, and newspapers. One of his secretary's jobs was to find these papers and save them until they were needed.

When the day was over, Einstein would often play music by Mozart and Bach on his violin. He played well and occasionally performed in public, to raise money for a cause he believed in. He also loved to play the piano—in fact, he called it "a necessity of his life" —but this he reserved for himself alone. He would never allow anyone to listen.

Although he was shy in public, Einstein liked to entertain his close friends and to discuss politics and philosophy, as well as physics, with them. Sometimes they played parlor games together and when the weather was good, he took them for rides in an eighteen-foot sailboat, his dearest possession. He seldom read for relaxation but admired the plays of Sophocles and Shakespeare and the novels of Dostoevski. The latter, he said, had given him "more pleasure than Gauss, the great mathematician."

Einstein was good-natured and found it hard to

say no to the many people who wanted him to write and speak, to sponsor movements and endorse issues. Often he would grant their requests, but, as Leopold Infeld wrote in his book on Einstein, the great physicist would "become suspicious if you came to him with a project that seemed to benefit him and not you." He was friendly and generous, but he was not naive.

All sorts of people with ideas also came to see Einstein. Sometimes they wanted him to listen to scientific theories that had not been accepted because, according to the theory-maker, they had not been understood. No matter how curious or unlikely these theories appeared to be, Einstein would give them his full attention. He understood that the most fundamental breakthroughs in physical knowledge at first seem incomprehensible.

If Einstein was to have any time for his own work, something had to be done about the stream of visitors. Until she died in 1936, his wife Elsa protected him. Then her daughter by a previous marriage came to live with Einstein and helped him in the same way.

Einstein was not cut off from the world, however, and frequently spoke his mind about issues he thought were important. One of these was Zionism. "The tragedy of the Jews," he said, "is that they are people of a definite historical type who lack the support of a community to hold them together." The Zionists' solution to this problem was to make Palestine a Jewish nation. Einstein helped them reach this goal although he did not like the religious orthodoxy or intense nationalism of the Zionists.

He continued to feel that war was the worst way to solve differences, but decided that an anti-Nazi war was justifiable and helped raise money for it in bond drives. His formula, $E = mc^2$, which had prompted other physicists to split the atom, was perhaps his most important war work. But in 1940 he made another contribution. At the instigation of the scientists who were trying to obtain the first chain reaction, he wrote to President Roosevelt about this new source of energy, which could be used in "extremely powerful bombs," and warned him that physicists in Germany were also working on nuclear fission. Einstein's importance was such that the government heeded his warning; other warnings had been put to one side.

Some of Einstein's opinions were not very popular at the time he stated them. When Senator Joseph McCarthy and other congressmen who were hunting for Communists required citizens to testify about their own and their friends' past activities and beliefs, Einstein said, "It is shameful for a blameless citizen to submit to such an inquisition [which] violates the spirit of the Constitution."

He continued to oppose militarism and pointed out that there are over a hundred colleges in the United States that offer courses on making war and only one or two that teach how to make peace.

Just before his death he joined the philosopher,

Bertrand Russell, and some other prominent people in a declaration against war. H-bombs can put an end to the human race, they said, and if there is another war, H-bombs are sure to be used, in spite of agreements between nations. Therefore, the declaration concluded, war itself must be prohibited.

Alfred Einstein died of a ruptured aorta on April 18, 1955. As he had requested, his brain and vital organs were removed for scientific study.

Since his death, Einstein's great fame has not diminished, but his reputation is changing. Each new generation of students finds his theories easier to understand. Each generation has fewer misconceptions about the universe to unlearn than had the generation before. As time passes and more and more people come to understand the significance of his work, Albert Einstein becomes less and less a symbol of the mysterious and the unknown.

CHAPTER 15

Harold C. Urey

In the fall of 1931, a young chemistry professor at Columbia University began to study a sample of liquid hydrogen. He had reason to believe, judging from recent research, that all hydrogen atoms were not the same. A tiny fraction had a mass that was twice as heavy as ordinary hydrogen atoms. The young professor, Harold Urey, had set out to isolate heavy hydrogen and prove that it did exist.

He boiled off the lighter atoms of the hydrogen sample; then put the concentrated residue in a vacuum tube and shot an electric current through it until it glowed brightly. Urey studied the lines of the spectrum and found what he was looking for: wave lengths of heavy hydrogen. The nuclei of ordinary hydrogen atoms contained one proton. These heavy atoms contained a neutron, as well as a proton, in their nuclei. Harold Urey named his discovery "deuterium" from the Greek word for "second."

For some time scientists had known that most elements are groups, or families, of atoms; and that certain members of each family have identical chemical properties but differ from other members in their physical properties, such as weight. The different members had been named "isotopes"; Harold Urey had discovered an isotope that was rare and valuable.

It was used as a tracer. Biologists could track deuterium as it passed through a living organism and in this way learn how hydrogen was used by cells.

Physicists used deuterons, atoms of deuterium, as projectiles to effect atomic transmutations and thus learn about atomic structure. And from the fusion of deuterium atoms came the power of H-bombs.

The man who isolated deuterium is both a chemist and a physicist, but he started out as a zoologist. Harold Clayton Urey was born in Walkerton, Indiana, on April 29, 1893. He was six years old when his father, a clergyman, died. His mother married again and Harold's stepfather was also a clergyman.

After he graduated from high school, Harold taught in some local country schools for several years. When his family moved to Montana, he followed them there and, in 1914, entered the University of Montana. He majored in zoology and graduated from college just before the United States entered World War I. Chemists were needed in war plants and Harold went to work in a Philadelphia chemical production plant. He never went back to zoology.

After a few years of working for industry, he decided to continue his education. He received a doctor's degree in chemistry from the University of California and then, on a fellowship from the American-Scandinavian Foundation, he went to Copenhagen to study under the great nuclear physicist, Niels Bohr.

Following his return to the United States in 1924, Harold Urey taught first at Johns Hopkins University and then at Columbia, where he began the experiments that brought him fame.

After he had isolated deuterium, Urey went to work on a way to produce it in quantity. Only one part in five thousand of ordinary hydrogen is deuterium and its isolation is a complicated process. A grant from Columbia made a plant for the production of heavy water (deuterium and oxygen) possible. The first pound of heavy water, which is used as a moderator in atomic reactors, cost sixty thousand dollars to produce.

For his isolation of deuterium, Harold Urey won the 1934 Nobel Prize in chemistry. He was modest about his achievement. "We just happened to get there first," he said. Some reporters who went to Columbia to interview him after his Nobel Prize was announced, found the square-faced, broad-shouldered young chemist looking quite distracted. A woodcock had just been caught on the window sill of the chemistry building, and Dr. Urey, worried about what might happen to it in the city, was arranging for the bird to be taken out into the country and released.

After he won the Nobel Prize, Harold Urey began to study the isotopes of nitrogen. In his laboratory on the ground floor of Havemeyer Hall—the old chemistry building on the Broadway side of the Columbia campus —he developed a mass-production method for partially separating these isotopes. The main section of his apparatus was a large, foil-wrapped, vertical steel pipe. When Urey decided that he needed a longer column, he broke a hole through the floor. Then he erected a thirty-five-foot pipe that extended from the ceiling of his laboratory down through a two-story vault underneath.

When Urey succeeded in isolating nitrogen isotopes, he gave biologists some important tools. Now, as they traced the paths of these isotopes through living organisms, they could explore the way living creatures manufacture their own flesh out of the proteins they eat.

Next Harold Urey turned to oxygen and carbon and discovered isotopes of these elements. By 1938 he had obtained isotopes of the four elements that, in various compounds, form approximately 96 per cent of living tissue—hydrogen, nitrogen, carbon, and oxygen.

His experiments with carbon-13, a stable isotope of carbon, show that research chemists may lead dangerous lives. The apparatus for these experiments contained enough poison to kill everyone in the laboratory. For protection, Urey kept his equipment in a vacuum, with the internal pressure lower than that of the outside air. In case of leaks, the air would be forced in, instead of gases seeping out. As an additional precaution, Urey kept canaries, just as miners do, to warn of poisonous gas.

As a result of his experiments, Urey succeeded in producing carbon isotopes by a method more than one hundred times faster than any previously devised. His process had an output of one hundred milligrams in twenty-four hours and produced a heavy-carbon concentration of 22 per cent. The new material was very expensive. If carbon in coal came at the price—$400 an ounce, exclusive of labor and apparatus—coal would cost $12,800,000 a ton.

In 1940 Urey announced that he had isolated isotopes of still another element—sulphur. His method of producing them, which involed a 150-foot tube, made these isotopes available in sufficient quantity and at a reasonable price for biological experiments and industrial procedures.

Harold Urey won many honors for his work: the Davy Medal of the Royal Society of London, the Franklin Medal of the Franklin Institute, the Willard Gibbs Medal of the American Chemical Society. He was appointed executive officer of Columbia's chemistry department.

During the years Urey was at Columbia, he lived

in Leonia, New Jersey. He had married Frieda Daum while he was teaching at Johns Hopkins and they had four children. It was largely due to his wife's efforts that Urey kept his daily schedule; to his students, the short, husky professor was all the things that absent-minded professors are supposed to be. He lectured to the wrong class in the wrong room. He wore mismated shoes to his office. He even returned in the afternoon wearing the same shoes—this time with one of them shined.

Aside from absent-mindedness, Harold Urey has few idiosyncrasies. But he does have hobbies. He draws charcoal portraits. He plays the piano by ear. And every six months he switches habits—from smoking to gum chewing, then back to smoking again.

In 1941, when the United States government's atomic program got under way, Harold Urey, well known for his ability to organize research, was called in to help. His method of separating fissionable U-235 from the rest of uranium was the one used at Oak Ridge, Tennessee, to produce A-bomb material.

During the war years, Urey's friends noticed that he looked different. He had always been a serious man; now, overworked, tired, and worried about the weapon he was helping to produce, he looked years older than he was.

When Urey saw atomic bombs used to destroy Japanese cities, he decided that these weapons were too dangerous to be controlled by individual nations. International control, he thought, was the only way to prevent misuse of atomic bombs, which could annihilate modern society. Although Urey had helped produce the atomic bomb he felt no guilt about it. "Atomic energy is in nature," he said. "It can't be concealed. Scientists can't prevent modern war by refusing to do scientific work. The solution is political."

Therefore Dr. Urey began to talk to politicians. He was not cut out to be a lobbyist and felt ill at ease when talking in congressional committee rooms but, as he put it, "I know the bomb can destroy everything we hold valuable, and I get a sense of fear that disturbs me in my work."

Therefore Dr. Urey continued to speak out. America, he warned, had no corner on nuclear weapons, no real secrets, no defense. Therefore, he argued, America must belong to one world, or it might belong to none.

When the war ended, Harold Urey's research took a new tack. At the Enrico Fermi Institute, in Chicago, and later at the University of California, his studies concerned such things as cosmic rays, the temperatures of the earth in prehistoric times, and the origin and constitution of the earth and moon.

In 1958 he was appointed to the National Research Council's Space Science board, which studied the problems and progress of the United States' research in space.

Harold Urey's theory about the moon and its formation was published in 1959. He pictured the moon in a radically different way than scientists had in the past, but his picture was in accord with recent information. For many years astronomers have believed the moon to be cold and dead. But in 1956 astronomers in Russia, England, and the United States observed a cloud on the moon's surface which spectrograms confirmed was gas discharged from a crater. According to Urey's theory, developed with two other University of California physicists, Walter M. Elsasser and M. G. Rochester, the moon was formed from masses of different density, which have never melted. If so, some parts of the moon's interior would be denser than others, making for a hot interior and a shifting surface, from which gases might sometime be discharged.

The study of the moon is far removed from zoology. Harold Urey's career in science, which began with zoology and went on to include physics and chemistry, has branched out into astrophysics. His multifold achievements do much to refute the view, popular today, that modern science is so complex that no one can venture beyond his own specialty.

CHAPTER 16

Herman Mark

"The molecular engineers are just getting started. Give them time."

When Dr. Herman Mark said this, he was talking about some of the changes his science will make in the future. He spoke of jet planes and missiles made of synthetic plastics that are as strong as or stronger than steel, far lighter, and able to stand temperatures up to five hundred degrees Centigrade; of adhesives that will altogether replace the screws and rivets that hold these jets and missiles together. He said that someday even skyscrapers and bridges will be made of plastics and would be glued together with other synthetic plastics.

And molecular engineers, Dr. Mark continued, may also make changes in the human body. Already a serum has been created that performs many of the functions of blood; in the future is the real possibility of engineered molecules that can replace red blood cells. Other molecular engineers are concerned with chromosomes, the cell parts that determine inherited characteristics. There is reason to think that these scientists might find a way to remove the cause of inherited defects.

"Polymer chemistry" is the official name of Dr. Mark's science, though "molecular engineering" describes it more meaningfully. Out of polymer chemistry, a science that only got under way in the twentieth century, have already come substances that have entirely changed the look, feel, properties, and price of things we use every day. To name just a few of these synthetic substances and one of the products made from each, there are the styrenes (toys), the vinyls (phonograph records), the acrylics (brush handles); polyethylene (squeeze bottles), buna S and buna N (tires), rayon, Orlon, and Dacron (clothing).

In the creation of every one of these synthetics, Herman F. Mark has played an important role. He is at the same time one of the highest paid consultants to industry in the United States, editor of the journal on which polymer chemists rely for the latest and most complete information, and professor at the Polymer Research Institute, the academic nerve-center of his science, which he founded himself and still heads. And he has written fourteen books and more than four hundred articles, headed a dozen scientific committees, and advised three branches of the United States government.

Dr. Mark's accomplishments do not stop here. A crack skier, he fought in the Austrian ski troops and, during the First World War, led his men to victory in a major campaign. He was later captured by the enemy and escaped, disguised as an English soldier.

When World War II came, Mark made another escape, this time from the Nazis and with his life savings, instead of himself, in disguise. In the United States, where he came to live, he found a way to construct a thousand-ton aircraft carrier made of ice, which was built.

The man who has been able to crowd so much into one lifetime is, as one might expect, uncommonly energetic and possesses remarkable mental abilities. For instance, Herman Mark is able to recall most of what he has read, complete with page numbers. Even more impressive to those who work with him is his ability to think about two—or more—things at the same time.

Herman Mark's two young secretaries at the Polytechnic Institute of Brooklyn, where he has his office, hear him humming entire scores of operas as he works with his slide rule. They say that often while he is discussing an aspect of chemistry with a scientist who comes to see him, he will work on computations of his own that have nothing to do with the conversation—without missing a word that his visitor utters, or a formula. Then the telephone will ring—another scientist is calling for some information—and Dr. Mark will sometimes ask his visitor to keep talking while he gives the man on the phone some data and continues his own computations with the slide rule, perfectly tuned in on all three lines of thought at once.

With so much going on in Dr. Mark's head, one might assume that he is rather unaware of other things —people, for instance. But this is not the case. When Dr. Mark warmly asks someone he meets, "How *are* you," he means it. Invariably he wants to know all about the health and well-being of the people he works with, and his students and co-workers come to him often for personal, as well as scientific, advice.

Herman Mark is a gay, convivial man, fond of parties, games, good food, wine, and singing. Indeed, his gaiety and good humor are so great that he is apt to overlook the formalities that go along with scholarly life. He greets his acquaintances as "Doctor" or "Professor," whether the person is an undergraduate student or the dean of Brooklyn Polytechnic, and has been known to address his secretaries as "Dear, darling super-secretaries."

Once when Dr. Mark ran into a fellow-scientist at a scholarly convention, where polite remarks on one another's latest work are the rule, he greeted the man warmly, told him that he had not yet read his latest book—but that he had weighed it and "it is clearly one of considerable importance."

Dr. Mark's good humor may help to explain why

he gets so much done. He is not at all fussy about where he works and is just as happy to check a formula while he sits on a park bench, flies in a plane, or waits in a bus station, as he is when he works at his own desk. Since his jobs as consultant to E. I. du Pont de Nemours and Company, the Polaroid Corporation, and Standard Oil of Indiana require that he be on the road three or four days out of every week, this flexibility comes in handy. So does his ability to get along with only a few hours' sleep and to get that sleep wherever he happens to be.

Morton M. Hunt, writing in *The New Yorker* magazine, has described Dr. Mark's habits when he is on the road. The scientist's plane will land—at Midway Airport, in Chicago, for instance, at three o'clock in the morning—and Dr. Mark will break into a brisk run as soon as he steps off the landing platform. Carrying two bulky brief cases, but not at all winded, white-haired, pink-cheeked Dr. Mark reaches the airline's waiting room and goes directly to a particular couch, which he knows is the most comfortable. From one of his brief cases he takes a small foam-rubber pillow in a clean pillow case, places it under his head, and—despite noise, lights, and staring passers-by—promptly goes to sleep.

Two hours later, at five A.M., Dr. Mark wakes up, feeling very fit; hurries off to the airport washroom, where he shaves; then returns to his couch. There he writes letters or edits an article for his *Journal of*

Polymer Science for a few hours, and then has a light breakfast at the airport coffee shop. At eight A.M., a car from Standard Oil of Indiana arrives to take him to their office. Dr. Mark trots briskly to meet the car, ready for a long day of meetings, conversations with research men, and plant inspections.

The energetic Herman Mark, who was born in Vienna, Austria, in 1895, began running to get places early in life. Every weekday he would cover the two miles from his home to school at a good pace; then, whenever he saw the chance, get into a game of soccer or tennis. Herman's father—a physician, who was born a Jew but later became a Lutheran—wanted his son to learn to play the piano, and so did Mrs. Mark. But whenever it was time for a lesson, Herman saw to it that he was far away, playing soccer or running around and around the cinder track at school.

When Herman was twelve years old, he saw something that had a profound effect on the rest of his life. One of his school friends, a boy named Gerhard Kirsch, took him on a tour of the University of Vienna's large chemistry laboratory, where Gerhard's father did research. Herman had never been very interested in chemistry, but when he saw a full-scale laboratory with all its intricate contraptions, he knew suddenly and with certainty that he must someday be a chemist. "I didn't have the slightest idea what was going on there," he says today, "but it made an enormous impression."

Before long Herman and his friend Gerhard had a small laboratory of their own. They had spent their savings on chemicals and equipment and talked Mrs. Mark into letting them set up the lab in Herman's bedroom. There they began a series of noisy, bad-smelling experiments while Mrs. Mark worried about the sudden disintegration of her towel supply.

In his first laboratory, Herman picked up some basic techniques. He borrowed chemistry textbooks from Gerhard, who was several years older, studied them, and soon had an understanding of chemistry that was advanced for his age.

When he finished school, Herman decided to enter compulsory military service and get that over with before continuing his education. He was still almost as interested in sports as he was in chemistry (a year before, when he was only seventeen, he had played on the national soccer league of Austria) and so he joined a mountain regiment, which required skiing and mountain climbing—two things he did well and hugely enjoyed.

Young Mark was having quite a good time in the army when, in the summer of 1914, the First World War began, and his regiment was sent to the dangerous Russian front. There he won a number of decorations for bravery and once, when his outfit was ordered to retreat as fast as possible, his fleetness and endurance saved his life. He retreated the ten-mile distance to safety at a fast run.

A large majority of the men in Herman's outfit were killed, wounded, or captured at the Russian front. Herman was wounded in the ankle by a piece of shrapnel and sent home to a hospital in Vienna, where he spent many of the long hours in bed reading chemistry books. Much to his comrades' surprise, he continued to study chemistry when he returned to the front lines. For three and a half years he fought on the Italian front, combining perilous missions, for which he won more medals, with scientific study, which he found just as relaxing as the more customary off-duty pastimes of soldiers.

In 1918, Mark, now a lieutenant, led three hundred men on a mission to retake a ridge called Zugna Torta that the Italians and Austrians had been fighting over for a long time. After a hard battle, Mark's men won the ridge. It was a major victory and Herman Mark was given the Leopolds Orden, Austria's highest honor.

A few months later the Austrian army was defeated by the Italians, and Mark was among those taken prisoner. At the Italian prison camp where he was interned, he used the free time he had suddenly acquired to study Italian, French, and English.

Six months later, when Mark learned that his father was very sick, he decided that the time had come to escape from prison camp and go home. So he faked a fight with another prisoner, and the authorities sent him, with one guard, to a disciplinary camp, which is just what he had hoped would happen. On the way to the camp, Mark, with the help of the money he had saved from his army pay, persuaded his guard to disappear.

As part of his escape plan, Lieutenant Mark had asked one of the cooks at the prison camp to buy him some brass buttons and a needle and thread. Now, free of his guard, he hastened to a railroad station washroom and quickly removed the green buttons on his uniform, which identified him as an Austrian soldier, and substituted the brass buttons. Then, hoping that he would pass for a British private, he got on a train that was heading north, toward Austria. Unfortunately, Mark found himself in a compartment with a real British soldier, an officer, who eyed the young man suspiciously.

At this point, Lieutenant Mark decided that honesty would be the best policy and he explained to the Englishman that he was trying to escape to Austria. Although the English had been fighting with the Italians against the Austrians, the officer, following the English tradition of fair play, made no trouble for Mark. "Good show," he told him. "Carry on."

When the train got close to the Italian border, Mark decided that it would be safer to get off and go the rest of the way to Austria on foot. This he did, enjoying his walk through the Alps and arriving home to find that his father was much better and that the peace treaty had been signed, ending World War I.

Three years later, in 1922, Herman Mark was in

Germany. He had completed his education at the University of Vienna, had married a young Viennese girl named Mary Schramek, and then had gone to Germany, where at first he taught at the University of Berlin and later took a position at the Kaiser Wilhelm Institute. There basic research was being done by an array of famous scientists, among them Einstein, Meitner, Planck, and Von Laue. Young Mark was impressed by the new territories these scientists were mapping out. He decided to take up physical chemistry, where he saw opportunities to explore some new territory himself.

"I realize," Mark says today, "how much I was influenced by the people I met then. Of course, when I was under these influences, I didn't know it. It's only later that you recognize these things."

Before Mark had been at the Kaiser Wilhelm Institute very long, he was assigned a difficult problem. This was to discover the size and shape of the molecules that make up hemp and find out how these molecules are arranged. Hemp is a cellulose, one of the organic substances, like meat, rubber, silk, and wool. Very little was known about these organic substances because they could not be analyzed with the usual techniques of chemistry. When cellulose is heated, for example, it does not melt, but becomes hard and decomposes. And it cannot be dissolved, except by chemicals that change it into another kind of substance altogether.

If Mark could discover the molecular structure of hemp, a new area of knowledge would be opened up.

He tackled the problem with enthusiasm and before long decided to try a completely new method of investigation.

The Nobel-Prize-winning physicist Max Von Laue had discovered that when a beam of X-rays was trained on a crystalline substance, it was deflected by the molecules. This caused a pattern to appear on film, a pattern that hinted at the molecular structure of the crystalline substance.

Although there was every reason to think that soft, flexible hemp was *not* composed of crystals, Mark and the scientists on his team decided to expose it to X-rays on a chance. To their surprise, the X-ray film recorded a pattern. Mark repeated this experiment, using cotton and other substances that are composed mainly of cellulose. Again patterns appeared on the film. He worked till late at night in the X-ray room with a research team that included the now well-known scientists Leo Szilard, Eugene Wigner, and Rudolf Brill. Mrs. Mark— "Mimi" as everyone called her—sent quantities of cake and coffee to the laboratory to sustain the team through the long night hours.

Before long, experiments by the Mark team and others revealed that cellulose was made of giant molecules, which in turn were made of long chains of smaller molecules. In cellulose, the molecular chains were straight and lay side by side. At certain points they were bound together, and it was these points that resembled crystals and made patterns on X-ray film.

Mark's discoveries about cellulose, which led later to the development of rayon, came to the attention of industrialists who saw possibilities of new products in the science of giant molecules, otherwise known as polymer chemistry. A director of the huge German firm of I. G. Farben came to Mark and offered him an excellent salary to head a research laboratory at Farben. The job and the salary suited Mark, who has always enjoyed having money and has never been ashamed to admit it.

For several years chemists at Farben had been tinkering with some mysterious, gummy substances called resins. It was known that the resins were composed of giant molecules, but that was about all that was known. Through trial and error, chemists had found ways to make some useful plastics out of resins, but when they were successful, they had no idea why.

Herman Mark's approach was different: he began with theory. After carrying out a number of experiments, he began to understand how the giant molecules that make up resins differ from the giant molecules that make up cellulose. These differences explained why the resins are gummy while cellulose is flexible and strong.

By the time Mark was able to put his knowledge to practical use, the heads of I. G. Farben were becoming restless. They had spent a great sum of money on Mark's research and they had seen nothing profitable come out of it. Just when their patience was about to give out, Mark's laboratory produced a muddy substance that, when molded, became a clear, solid plastic. It was named polystyrene and soon was used for numerous articles, from toys of every kind to electrical insulation. Mark followed up this commercial success with other multi-useful synthetics, among them polyvinyl, polyacrylic, and buna N and buna S, the first synthetic forms of rubber.

Herman Mark was still working for I. G. Farben in 1932, when it began to look as if the Nazis would take over the German government. Because his father had been born a Jew, Mark was in a dangerous position. The Farben firm made no objection when he decided to leave Germany and return home to Austria.

At the University of Vienna, where Mark went to head the First Chemical Institute, he returned to theoretical work, relieved to be away from the pressure of I. G. Farben, but busy as ever. There was a laboratory he could use at the university, and he began a series of experiments aimed at discovering exactly what takes place chemically when giant-molecule synthetics are formed. He wanted to summarize into a fundamental set of laws, or equations, all the various bits of information that chemists had gathered through trial and error. This he succeeded in doing. An industrial chemist who wanted to create a new synthetic could use Mark's equations the way a cook uses a recipe. All the chemist had to do was to follow the equation-recipe; he could be sure that the resulting synthetic was exactly what he was trying to get.

In Austria, Herman Mark found another new job, one that suited him perfectly because it involved skiing. He became a member of the government's avalanche-warning commission. When an avalanche was reported, it meant that he could ski up a mountain to question observers about the weather conditions that had preceded the avalanche—and then ski down the mountain again.

In 1938, the Nazis again forced Mark to change countries and jobs. This time his escape was a close one. When the Germans invaded Austria, Mark, again because of his father's religion, was among the people who were arrested and taken to the Gestapo. After a night of questioning, he was released; soon afterwards he was told that he no longer had his job at the university.

Mark knew that the Nazis would never give him official permission to leave Austria. But after some delicate maneuvers, he managed to get, in exchange for a bribe, authorization for a short trip to Switzerland. He, of course, was planning a far more extensive trip and wanted to take with him the money he had saved. At that time there were strict inspections at the Austrian borders, and all money was usually confiscated by SS or SA guards. To solve this difficulty, Mark bought some platinum wire and bent it into coat hangers and his wife covered them with cloth. And so when Mark

drove his car across the Austrian border, it contained
—along with Dr. and Mrs. Mark, their two sons, and a
few pieces of luggage—some clothes suspended from
coat hangers.

In Switzerland Mark sold his coat hangers for four
thousand dollars and began to look, by letter, for a new
job and a new home. These he found in Canada, where
he became research director for a pulp manufacturer.
But he did not keep his new job for long. Research into
pulp-testing methods was not much of a challenge to
his abilities, and in Canada he felt far away from polymer research. In 1940 he accepted a position as consultant to du Pont and moved to the United States, to
Brooklyn, where, at the Polytechnic Institute, du Pont
had arranged for him to be a part-time professor. With
his loyal, inventive wife and two sons (who both grew
up to become physicists) he began a new life in the
United States.

When word got around that Mark was teaching at
Brooklyn Polytechnic, polymer chemists flocked there
to consult and study with him. Before long Mark persuaded Brooklyn Polytechnic to set up a branch devoted
to the study of giant molecules and the Polymer Research Institute was formed. It became the world center
of learning in polymer chemistry.

In 1941, a year after Mark had come to the United
States to live, he received a telephone call from a British
inventor named Geoffrey Pyke, the head of a top secret
war project called "Operation Habbakuk." Back in

Vienna, Mark had studied glaciers, another interest that stemmed from his love of skiing, and had published some articles about ice formation. The members of Operation Habbakuk thought he might be able to help them find a way to build an aircraft carrier made of ice. Such a craft, they hoped, would be unsinkable; it would contain refrigerating equipment to maintain the ice and to close up the holes with new ice, if the carrier was hit by a bomb or torpedo. The scheme had only one drawback: a direct torpedo hit or even a very rough sea would break up ordinary ice; the Habbakuk men wondered if Mark knew a way to solve this problem.

Herman Mark did. After some experiments in a cold-storage warehouse, where he worked in overcoat and ear muffs, he came up with a mixture of water and wood pulp that, when frozen, was far stronger than pure ice and had the additional advantage of melting at a slower rate.

A model aircraft carrier, sixty feet long and weighing one thousand tons, was built of Mark's ice and made a trial run, in 1943, on Jasper Lake in Canada. By this time, however, German submarines were far less of a threat, so a fleet of icy aircraft carriers was never built and the test model was left to melt away.

Mark's knowledge of snow and ice was again put to use when the Army asked him to assist the team that developed a snowmobile called the "weasel," and later he helped design the DUKW, an amphibious truck.

When the war was over, Herman Mark found new

outlets for the energy he had left over from his perennial occupations of teacher, editor, consultant, administrator, and scientist. He headed a scientific planning committee for the Weizmann Institute of Science, in Israel, and a wood-utilization committee for the United Nations. But in Mark's opinion his most important work has been to instruct, encourage, and materially aid young up-and-coming molecular engineers.

In recent years new ways have been found to build giant molecules. For example, inorganic chemical groups can be inserted in the chains of small molecules that form the giant molecules, or whole new branches can be attached to the chains. By these means, and by using heat and radiation, chemists are able to change the giant molecules in just about any way they wish. This knowledge gives them creative power, the power to invent materials. As Mark puts it, "Starting from a need for some material of specified properties, we are in a position to create a new material tailored to fit that need." It is even possible, he goes on to say, "to create synthetics with properties never known before."

Mark's unique combination of jobs made him an essential link between research chemists and industries that wanted new products and profits. As consultant to industries that produce synthetics, he agitated for more basic research, for using the abilities of chemists on long-range projects that will pay off in new knowledge and probably, though not right away, in profits. And as teacher and friend of polymer chemists, Mark introduced them to people who could help them, found them challenging jobs in basic research that paid well, and, of course, gave them his knowledge of polymer chemistry, both theoretical and applied.

"After you are sixty-five years old," said Dr. Mark, "it makes little difference whether you write one or two more technical papers. Now it's the human influence that counts. The important thing for me to do is to help these young men onto the launching pad."

And when they leave the launching pad, Dr. Mark's molecular engineers travel to a new frontier of science, a frontier that is expanding as fast as that of outer space.

"The molecular engineers are just getting started," says Dr. Mark. "Give them time."

CHAPTER 17

Enrico Fermi

On the morning of December 2, 1942, scientists, wearing overalls blackened with graphite dust, gathered about a huge pile of what looked like bricks of coal. The pile dominated a spacious room, almost reaching its twenty-six-foot ceiling. Walls, ceiling, and floor were greasy and black as pitch.

Once University of Chicago students had played squash in this room under the grandstand of their football stadium, Stagg Field. Now the squash court housed one of the greatest secrets of World War II, the first atomic pile. Top-rank scientists from the United States and Europe had been working on it for a long time.

On this morning in December, university students and faculty went about their usual tasks completely unaware of the crucial event about to take place in the squash court. For today scientists would learn whether man could release sustained nuclear energy and whether, once released, he could control it.

Little by little the pile of graphite bricks, some embedded with uranium, had grown larger. The scientists had calculated that when the pile reached a certain "critical" size, the fissioning uranium would set off a chain reaction, which would grow in intensity. Then for the first time, man would have at his disposal energy that did not come from the sun.

The scientists believed that they could control the intensity of a chain reaction and harness it to work for them. Their calculations and measurements had told them that this was possible. But they could not be absolutely certain of what would happen today, because they were going to do something that had never been done before.

That is why three young men, half-jokingly called the "suicide squad," were perched on a platform above the pile. Their job was to flood the pile with a solution of cadmium if the chain reaction got out of control. They were there just in case.

The men who gathered in the ex-squash court that day were tense; their chief, Enrico Fermi, was not. The stocky, short-legged man, with sensitive features and discerning eyes, went about his work with deliberation. Periodically, he checked the instruments that recorded the pile's radioactivity, then pulled out his slide rule, which he always carried with him, and calculated something.

Fermi was sure that his mathematics were correct and that the pile would act just as he predicted it should. This man, nicknamed "Pope" and "Admiral" by the scientists who worked under him, had reason to trust his own judgment. Again and again he had demonstrated his ability to reduce the most complex problem to its essentials and then to arrive at the correct solution. He had proved himself a master of both theoretical and experimental physics, something no other contemporary physicist can claim. His discoveries about the atom were so various and so important that his life history is also, in large part, the history of atomic energy.

Enrico Fermi had not always been considered brilliant. His second-grade teacher at school thought he was rather slow. Once she asked the class to write down some products made of iron. Enrico, who had noticed a sign, "Iron Bed Factory," on his way to school, wrote: "With iron one makes some beds." The word *some* in this sentence showed that he understood that every bed was not made of iron, but his teacher did not recognize this. She gave him a very low grade and Enrico's mother began to worry about her son's intelligence. Fermi's ability to think with precision, to go right to the root of the matter, eliminating the nonessentials, was often misunderstood when he was very young.

Enrico Fermi was a shy, thoughtful boy. He was born in Italy on September 29, 1901, the last of a family of three. Alberto Fermi, his father, came from a family which had always farmed; Alberto was the first to leave home and find a different occupation. Although he had no higher education to speak of, he became an administrator on a railroad, quite an important position. He married an elementary-school teacher, Ida De Gattis, and they settled down in Rome to raise a family—first Maria, then Giulio, then Enrico.

The last two Fermi children were born very close together, and Mrs. Fermi was unable to take care of two babies. So Giulio and Enrico were sent away to the country, where they were tended by a nurse; and Enrico, who was not a strong child, did not come home to stay until he was two-and-a-half years old. On his first day at home, his sister remembers, he cried a lot, probably because he missed his nurse and the only home he had ever known. But when his mother spoke firmly to him and told him he must stop, he did as she asked, and from then on accepted her authority, which was quite rigid.

Giulio was only a year older than Enrico; the brothers were inseparable. They were both very bright and they liked to do the same things. They were interested in airplane engines, and were always designing and building motors—motors that worked. The adults who saw their drawings and models were astonished. They did not look at all like the work of children.

Giulio was not shy, like Enrico; he was gay and warmhearted and everyone was drawn to him. But neither Giulio nor Enrico made other close friends at school. They had no need to.

Then, when Enrico was fourteen, there was a tragedy. During a minor throat operation, Giulio died. No one, not even the doctor, knew the cause. Mrs. Fermi wept and was inconsolable. Enrico could not cry. He had lost his dearest and only friend. Everything he saw, everything he loved best to do, reminded him of his brother.

One day, a week after Giulio's death, Enrico found his way back to the hospital. All he did was walk past it. He wanted to see whether he would be able to control the emotion he felt when he saw the place where Giulio had died.

Now Enrico began to study, first mathematics, then physics. He read constantly. He was not satisfied until he found explanations for the things he observed that puzzled him—the movement of a top, for instance. What, he wondered, causes the upper part of a top, to move around in a circle when it is slowing down?

One day at school Enrico found a friend, a boy his own age named Enrico Persico, who was also preoccupied with science. Together they tackled the problem of the top, thinking and talking of nothing else for weeks. They did not know the two equations that would have helped them. Using their limited knowledge of mechanics, they struggled with the problem until they worked out for themselves the physical laws that govern tops, or any gyroscope.

Enrico's great interest in physics was encouraged and guided by a friend of his father's. This man, Ingegner Amidei, saw the boy's knowledge grow until it surpassed his own. He encouraged Enrico to apply for a scholarship to a school in Pisa for outstanding students, and the boy won it with ease. Seventeen-year-old Enrico set out for Pisa, leaving behind him the gloomy atmosphere that had settled on his family since Giulio's death.

Fermi was happy at the Reale Scuola Normale of Pisa. While there he met Franco Rasetti, and they became friends for life. Rasetti also was a brilliant student. He had a great gift for biology, which he had loved since he was four years old. But, like Fermi, he had chosen to study physics. This was because he found physics extremely difficult and he wanted to prove to himself that he could overcome any obstacle.

At Pisa, once the home of Galileo, Fermi and Rasetti learned a great deal of physics, but not in class. Fermi soon discovered that he already knew most of the things covered in his courses. Fortunately, his physics teacher gave him the run of the laboratory, and Fermi began to study the quantum theory on his own.

Before very long, he knew more than the physics professor. One day this gentleman came to Fermi and asked the young man to teach him about Einstein's relativity. "I am an ass," said the teacher on that occasion, "but you think clearly and I can always understand things when you explain them."

Fermi received his doctor's degree, with highest honors, when he was twenty-one. Before getting the degree, he was required to speak about his work before eleven examiners. As Fermi talked, the examiners yawned and looked stupefied, gazing with bewilderment at the student. It was quite clear that they did not understand what the young man was talking about.

Although Fermi had done so well in school, he had no way of knowing how he measured up to scientists in other countries. Italy had produced no great physicists for many years, and there were few physics teachers of merit in Italian universities. For this reason he did not feel very proud of the honors he had won and decided to go to Germany, to Göttingen, where promising young physicists from many nations had gathered to study with one of the world's foremost scientists, Max Born.

Fermi was the only Italian who was studying physics at Göttingen; he felt very foreign and his childhood shyness returned. Professor Born did not realize how much his student needed a few encouraging words. Unfortunately, Fermi could not guess what Born revealed thirty years later: that the learned professor was rather awed by the young Italian with his obvious ability and penetrating comments, that Born would have appreciated a pat on the back from Fermi!

Fermi returned to Italy and a year later again

went abroad to study, this time in Leiden, Holland. There the learned Professor Ehrenfest told Fermi that he had the makings of a good physicist. This was the affirmation he needed.

In 1924, Fermi began to earn his living as a teacher. First he taught mathematics at the University of Rome; then he went to Florence, where he continued to teach while he worked on a theory.

An important frontier had just been opened up in physics. Fermi had read with keen interest about discoveries concerning the energies of atoms and the particles that make them up. Now he worked out a mathematical system that described and predicted the behavior of molecules in an ideal gas. Fermi's work led to an understanding of the conduction of electricity in metals, and his mathematical system, or statistics, became a valuable tool in physics. He could have spent the rest of his life using these statistics to solve various problems, but he preferred to move on to new frontiers.

When Senator Orso Corbino, the head of the physics department at the University of Rome, read Fermi's statistical theory, he acted at once. Corbino was a man with a mission: to put the University of Rome on the map as a world center of physics. Corbino himself was the only physicist of note to come from Italy in a quarter of a century. He was painfully aware of the low standing of his own physics department and was on the lookout for brilliant teachers. He hired

Fermi's college friend, Franco Rasetti, and saw to it that Fermi, a youthful professor of twenty-four, was added to his staff.

Corbino had chosen well. Fermi's work soon brought him world-wide recognition and his classes attracted students. The young professor was able to reduce complicated theories to their fundamentals and explain them in simple language. Sometimes during informal teaching sessions he would bring up one of the problems that had come up in his own work. Using the blackboard, he would demonstrate how he picked out the essential factors of the problem, how he eliminated others. In this way, the students could see for themselves the way a scientist attacks a problem.

Fermi always made it a point to take time off from his teaching and studies for exercise. A certain part of one's time should be devoted to work, he thought; another part to exercise. The important thing in life was to keep in good physical shape and spend one's energy where it counted. He was not interested in lost causes or in speculation for its own sake. Getting things done was what mattered to him. He was a very rational, down-to-earth young man.

One of Fermi's companions on the hikes and mountain climbs he prescribed for himself, and enjoyed, was a student at the university, a girl named Laura Capon. She had first met Fermi when he was twenty-two and she was sixteen; he had seemed very old to her. Now he was a full professor, she a student.

Laura was surprised to discover that they could still joke and talk freely together.

In 1928 Laura and Enrico were married. Mrs. Fermi has since revealed that Enrico was almost late for the ceremony. While she was waiting for him to appear, he was at home, sewing. At the last minute he had discovered that the sleeves of his new wedding shirt were too long. Characteristically, he had analyzed the situation and then done the logical thing: found a sewing machine and used it to take large tucks in the shirt sleeves. He arrived at Laura's home just in time to make it to the wedding.

Many years later Laura Fermi wrote a book about her life with the great physicist. She called the book *Atoms in the Family* and in it told many amusing and dramatic stories about her husband, his work, and what it is like to go through life with a man who is almost infallible about everything.

When Fermi was twenty-eight years old, he was chosen to represent physics in the newly formed Royal Academy of Italy, a great honor for someone so young. Now he had a title, "His Excellency," if he cared to use it. The down-to-earth Fermi did not care to. "What possible use can I have for this title?" he wanted to know. "If a clerk who was waiting on me should ask who I am, and I replied, '*His* Excellency Fermi,' it would sound foolish. I'm sure I wouldn't get faster service either. If anything, I would prefer to be called '*My* Excellency Fermi'!"

At this period of his life, Fermi was doing theoretical work on the behavior of one particle in the electrical field of another. Then, in 1932, his interests shifted to another new frontier, nuclear physics. Two years later he completed his theory of beta decay, which physicists consider a stroke of genius.

This theory accounts for the disintegration of a radioactive nucleus when an electron (beta particle) and a particle called a neutrino are emitted. The beta-decay theory has had a profound influence on nuclear physics, but, like Fermi's statistics, it is not well known outside the scientific world. The reason for this is that both theories are so advanced that they do not make much sense to anyone but a physicist; and even physicists had trouble understanding the beta-decay theory at first, because the ideas involved were so unfamiliar.

The history of the beta-decay theory illustrates what one physicist calls Fermi's "uncanny hunches" and his ability to decide which experimental results were misleading and which made it necessary to discard an old theory and invent a new one. In Fermi's beta-decay theory he described the behavior of various nuclear particles and forces. Little was known about the nucleus when he worked out his theory, and his descriptions were based, not on laboratory research, but on calculations and a kind of intuition.

Then, after Fermi's theory appeared, scientists began to do more experiments on beta decay and to gather information about it. Twenty years later they thought they knew enough to disprove parts of Fermi's theory.

Fermi thought not. "These experiments are misleading," he would say. "They are not precise enough to be considered decisive tests of my theory." And he continued to believe that he would be proved correct in the end.

That is what happened. Scientists continued to formulate new theories about the nucleus and to test them in experiments, experiments which became increasingly elaborate and exact. In 1957 they arrived at a comprehensive understanding of beta decay and, surprisingly, it confirmed Fermi's "uncanny hunches." His theory of beta decay is accepted in its essentials today.

The ideas presented in Fermi's theory were considered so novel in 1934 that a leading scientific magazine refused to publish it. Fermi decided that now would be a good time to try something entirely new, something he had been wanting to do.

In 1934 physicists knew that they had to have more concrete information about the nucleus of the atom. They would not be able to make more theories until the nucleus had been studied in many further experiments. Fermi was excited about this new frontier in physics. He had some ideas for a series of experiments and he did not want to wait until someone else, trained in laboratory work, gathered the information he needed. So although up until now his work had been done almost entirely on paper, he decided to conduct the experiments himself. It was as if a lawyer trained himself to be a doctor so that he could get the medical information he needed to win a case.

Fermi began to build a Geiger counter—they couldn't be bought at that time—and to plan his experiments. He had read about an important discovery made by Mme. Curie's daughter, Irène, and Frédéric Joliot, Irène's husband. Fermi had some interesting ideas about their discovery.

The Joliot-Curies, as the couple were called, had bombarded aluminum with alpha particles, which are given off by radium and other radioactive substances. When the alpha bullets penetrated the nuclei of aluminum atoms, particles of the nuclei were expelled violently and the aluminum was transformed into another element, an unstable, radioactive element. For the first time radioactivity had been produced artificially.

Fermi thought about this experiment. He knew that alpha particles had many disadvantages as atomic bullets. Because they have a positive electrical charge, they are attracted to the negatively charged electrons that surround the nucleus, and they are repelled by the positively charged nucleus—the target. Consequently, few alpha particles reach and enter the nucleus.

Perhaps, Fermi speculated, there is another particle that would work better. Two years before, James Chadwick had discovered the neutron, a particle found in the nucleus which has no electrical charge at all.

Now, Fermi reasoned, if instead of alpha particles, I used neutrons to bombard the elements, the chance of hitting the target would be much better. There might be some very interesting results.

A number of things had to be done before Fermi could begin to experiment. First he must have a source of neutrons. Luckily, he was able to borrow a gram of radium from the Bureau of Public Health in Rome; the radon gas given off by radium could be mixed with beryllium to produce neutrons. Then he must have samples of the elements he wished to bombard. This necessitated a good deal of shopping and looking around, something that did not interest him at all. But before long he had a team and they shared the work.

Corbino had been successful in attracting other bright young men to his physics department, and Emilio Segré and Edoardo Amaldi, as well as Fermi's old friend, Rasetti, were eager to get in on the experiments, which looked exciting. Rasetti became Fermi's second in command, Amaldi took over the electronics, and Segré was willing to shop for elements.

The team needed a chemist too. One day a young man named D'Agostino, who happened to be a chemist, stopped in at the lab, just to see what was going on. He was about to take a train to Paris, where he had a fellowship in Irène Curie's laboratory, but Fermi's experiment looked interesting. The young men were enthusiastic about the possibilities of their work; there was excitement in the air. D'Agostino had his train ticket extended three times and finally gave up going to Paris altogether.

The team needed all the help they could get. At one point they even talked the twelve-year-old brother of one of their students into lending a hand. They convinced him that making neat paper containers to hold the elements was interesting and vital work!

Fermi planned his experiment systematically. He wanted to bombard all the ninety-two elements then known to man. The elements had been organized into a Periodic Table by the Russian chemist, Mendeléev, and assigned numbers according to their atomic weights. Fermi decided to begin with the first element on the Periodic Table, hydrogen, and continue through the last element, uranium.

When all the preparations had been completed, he began to bombard his sample of hydrogen with neutrons. Nothing happened. Helium was not available, so he tried the next element, lithium. Again no results. Then he tried beryllium and so on until he had tested six more elements. But still nothing happened; they all failed to react to neutron bombardment.

In spite of these depressing results, he continued, because, as Segré put it later, Fermi "knew for sure" that the experiment would work. The next element was fluorine. Fermi exposed it to the neutron source and the Geiger counter began to chatter. Success! Fluorine had become highly radioactive.

The team grew more and more excited as they

bombarded the elements that followed fluorine on the Periodic Table and produced radioactivity again and again. Radio-phosphorus and radio-cobalt, both now used for the treatment of cancer, were among the radioactive nuclei, called "Fermi atoms," that were discovered during the spring of 1934. Scientists all over the world focused their attention on the little laboratory in Rome as one dramatic experiment followed another and radioactive nuclei, more than sixty of them, were mass-discovered.

Fermi knew that when one of his neutrons entered the nucleus of an atom and became part of it, an electron was eventually expelled. In this way, the element's atomic number was increased by one, and it became an entirely different element, the one that came next on the Periodic Table. What would happen, he wondered, when the last element on the Periodic Table, uranium, was bombarded? Logically, uranium, element 92, would become element 93. But there *was* no element 93. Perhaps a new element, one never before found in nature, would be discovered!

When the time came to bombard uranium, Fermi and his team eagerly examined the results. They found that the experiment had produced three known isotopes, or forms, of uranium and a mysterious fourth element. It was not one of the elements close to uranium on the Periodic Table. Was it element 93? They thought it might be but could not be absolutely certain.

Fermi was a cautious man. He did not want to

announce publicly that a new element might have been discovered. But Senator Corbino, elated by the success of his physics department, hastened to tell the press. This embarrassed Fermi very much, both then and later.

Five years passed before Fermi found out what had *really* happened when he bombarded uranium. The result of the experiment was something more extraordinary than a new element, something that almost no one guessed at the time.

As Fermi and his team continued to work together, they came to know one another very well. They grew familiar with each other's weaknesses, joked about them, and became good friends. Their comradeship and high spirits made them an even better team. They criticized each other's ideas and worked at the peak of their abilities.

Senator Corbino called the young physicists his "boys," but they chose more exalted names for themselves: Rasetti was known as the "Cardinal Vicar"; Fermi, because he was infallible, was the "Pope." But the teammates behaved more like boys than church dignitaries. They were fond of jokes and of all kinds of games in which they could compete. They went swimming and mountain-climbing and played tennis together whenever they could. Once they even sailed toy boats—new gadgets on the market that were propelled by lighted candles—on Senator Corbino's goldfish pond.

Fermi was probably the most competitive member

of the team. On mountain climbs he was famous for always trying to keep in the lead and, when the mountain top was in sight, he would be sure to reach it before anyone else.

The team members kept up their exercise—and competition—when they were in the laboratory. Because the neutron source itself was radioactive (and therefore could affect the Geiger counter and confuse the experiment), it had to be kept far away from the counter. After bombardment, an element was carried down a long hall to the room where the counter was, so that the degree of radioactivity could be measured. Sometimes radioactivity was short-lived, and the physicists would have to run as fast as they could to make it to the counter in time. But even when there was no emergency, Amaldi and Fermi would dash down the corridor, trying to beat the other's time. Fermi always claimed that he could run the fastest, but his friends agree that this claim is not completely trustworthy. Fermi hated to lose a contest or a game.

But no one has ever questioned Fermi's ability to exhaust his teammates when it was a matter of work. He began in his study at five in the morning. There he would review the results of the day before and plan future experiments, so that he always had a very clear idea about what he wanted to accomplish during the current day. Invariably, he stopped his homework at exactly 7:30 A.M. (though he never consulted a clock, some mysterious mental process always told him the correct time) and arrived at the laboratory at eight. He remained there until one in the afternoon, took a break until three—often to play a fast game of tennis with Rasetti—and then returned to the lab for five more hours. There, his collaborators agree, he did at least twice as much work as anyone else.

One day at the laboratory a curious phenomenon was brought to Fermi's attention. Bruno Pontecorvo (a new team member who, in 1950, disappeared behind the Iron Curtain) and Amaldi had been observing some silver that had a neutron source inside it. The silver, they noticed, became a bit more radioactive when it was placed on a wooden table. Fermi was called in, and the team began to test the silver in every way they could think of, to see if other substances would affect its radioactivity. They finally tried paraffin, and the results were dramatic. When a neutron source embedded in paraffin was placed inside a hollow silver block, the silver became one hundred times more radioactive. The Geiger counter reacted with such a chatter that at first Segré thought it was broken!

Why did the silver act this way? Fermi had an idea, and when he went home for lunch, he worked out a hypothesis. Paraffin, he knew, contains a large amount of hydrogen (the wood of the table, a smaller amount). Perhaps, he reasoned, as our neutrons pass through the paraffin, they collide with protons, the particles that make up hydrogen nuclei and have the same weight as neutrons. These collisions would slow the neutrons down and make it easier for the silver atoms to capture them.

Fermi returned to the lab after lunch and told his team about the hypothesis. They immediately set out to test it. If it was correct, then other substances that contain large amounts of hydrogen would slow down neutrons and make them more effective bullets. Why not try H_2O?

They needed quite a lot of water for the experiment, more than the lab could provide. The team hesitated only an instant; then the solution came to them—Senator Corbino's goldfish pond! It was right behind the laboratory. They lost no time gathering up their equipment. Soon silver and neutron source were under water with the goldfish (which survived), and the Geiger counter was chattering again.

Artificial radioactivity had been vastly increased; Fermi's hypothesis was confirmed. He had discovered an extremely potent projectile, the slow neutron. This was to play a vital role in the development of nuclear energy.

The young men were excited that afternoon. As Segré puts it, "We all started to shout with our loud Italian voices, listing possible consequences and how to test them by experiments." At the end of the day, too elated to go home, they went over to the Amaldis' house to write up the experiment and continued to shout ideas at one another until late that night.

Fermi continued to experiment with the neutron

between 1934 and 1938, and his work brought fame and foreign students to the University of Rome, just as Senator Corbino had hoped. But meanwhile Fermi, who had been spending his summers teaching in the United States, had decided to leave Italy for good and settle in America. He had watched Mussolini's power grow and did not like what he saw.

One day, soon after returning from a summer in the United States, Fermi was driving with a friend from Rome to Florence. As they passed the Fascist slogans that had been painted on houses along the road, Fermi shouted them out, with an addition of his own:

" 'Mussolini is always right.' Burma Shave!

" 'To fight is necessary; to win is more necessary.' Burma Shave!"

The Fermis now had two children—a girl, Nella, born in 1931, and a boy, Giulio, born in 1936—and they did not want their children to be educated into Fascists. They had planned to leave for America in 1939. Then, in 1938, two dramatic events caused Mr. and Mrs. Fermi to revise their plans: Mussolini passed his first anti-Semitic laws, which were a threat to Mrs. Fermi, who was Jewish; and Fermi learned that he might receive the Nobel Prize.

Mrs. Fermi has described the day of November 10, 1938, when she and her husband were awakened early in the morning by the telephone. The operator informed them that at six that evening there would be a call from Stockholm, Sweden, for Professor Fermi.

Did this mean that Fermi had won the Nobel Prize? All day long Mr. and Mrs. Fermi speculated about it and when evening finally came, they sat down in the living room and nervously waited for the call. Shortly after six, the phone rang. It was a friend who had heard about the operator's warning and wanted to know whether Stockholm had called yet!

The Fermis settled down again and turned on the radio to pass the time. They tuned in a commentator, who announced that Mussolini had passed more anti-Semitic laws. The children of Jews could no longer attend public schools; the passports of Jews would be confiscated.

The phone rang again. It was the same friend. "Has Stockholm called yet?" she wanted to know.

At last the call from Stockholm came through. Fermi had won the Nobel Prize for "his identification of new radioactive elements and his discovery . . . of nuclear reactions affected by slow neutrons."

The award would be presented in Sweden next month. Mr. and Mrs. Fermi changed their plans and decided to emigrate right away. They would go to Sweden for the Nobel ceremonies and then continue on, to America.

They made careful, secret preparations for their journey. Fortunately, it was still possible for Mrs. Fermi to use her passport. They visited the United States consulate for permission to go to America to live and took the required examination.

There Fermi was asked to add 15 and 27. "Forty-two," the Nobel-Prize winner replied, with deliberation and pride.

Fermi had accepted a professorship at Columbia University, in New York. He told everyone but a few close friends that he would teach at Columbia for six months and then return to Rome.

One December morning the Fermis, their two children, and a nursemaid boarded the train for Stockholm. Mrs. Fermi relates that her husband appeared calm, even when a guard at the German border, who had taken their passports, seemed dissatisfied with them.

Nella Fermi, who was then eight years old, began to ask questions. Was something the matter? she wanted to know. Would they be sent back to Rome and Mussolini?

Enrico spoke to the guard in German and discovered what the trouble was. The guard had been searching their passports for a German visa, permission to enter the country. When the visa was pointed out to him, all was well; and the trip to Stockholm was completed safely.

The Fermis were royally received in Stockholm. When Gustavus V, the king of Sweden, handed Fermi the Nobel award, the physicist shook hands with the king. Italian Fascists were horrified when they learned that Fermi had not greeted the monarch with their official salute!

On the second day of 1939 the Fermis sailed into New York harbor. "We have founded the American branch of the Fermi family," said Enrico, as he greeted the New York skyline and the Statue of Liberty. Before long they were settled in Leonia, New Jersey, which their new friend, Harold Urey, recommended as a pleasant place to live.

There were many things for Enrico Fermi to learn about in the United States. One thing that fascinated him was the gadgets he found here and, although he was a thrifty man, he bought one piece of automatic equipment after another—everything from an electric saw to a step-on garbage can. These products of technology were proof, he thought, of man's continuing search for ways to save labor and better his existence. Fermi believed that, in a way, gadgets symbolized the promise of America.

Two weeks after the Fermis docked in New York harbor, another great scientist arrived from Europe, Niels Bohr. Bohr brought dramatic news with him: a team of German scientists had split the atom. When Fermi heard about this experiment, he understood what had really happened when he bombarded uranium five years ago.

At that time Fermi thought that his experiment might have produced a new element. Other scientists thought so too. Only one, a woman, had disagreed. A German chemist named Ida Noddack criticized Fermi's experiment in a letter to a scientific magazine. She thought that neutron bombardment of uranium atoms might cause the nuclei to break into fragments that were really forms of known elements. Scientists paid little attention to Ida Noddack's theory because they could not imagine that the neutron, a particle with no electrical charge, could do what none of the powerful atom-smashing machines had been able to achieve.

Two other women scientists proved that Ida Noddack was right. Irène Curie also was not quite satisfied with Fermi's results. She repeated his experiment and announced that neutron bombardment of uranium did not produce a *new* element; it produced something that closely resembled a *known* element, lanthanum, which has an atomic weight almost half that of uranium. This was correct, as far as it went, but Irène Curie did not recognize the crux of the matter.

The third woman was Lise Meitner. She, Otto Hahn, and Frederic Strassmann had been working on neutron bombardment of uranium, in Germany. When news of Irène Curie's experiment was published, Lise Meitner was no longer with the group. Because she was an Austrian Jewess, Germany was far too dangerous for Frau Meitner in 1938, and she had had to escape to a neutral country, Sweden. There Lise Meitner read about the experiment her teammates had just completed.

They, too, had repeated Fermi's experiment. They had bombarded uranium, with its atomic weight of about 238, and had obtained isotopes whose atomic weights were about 140 and 90. It was clear that the atoms had been broken almost in half, yet Hahn and Strassmann could not bring themselves to a conclusion which was, as they put it, "in opposition to all previous experience in nuclear physics."

Lise Meitner was less conservative. She pored over the details of her collaborators' experiment. Then, with the advice of her nephew, Otto Frisch, she arrived at a theory that satisfactorily explained what had happened: the uranium atoms had split; and since the mass of the pieces that were formed was much less than the mass of uranium, it was clear that a large amount of energy had been produced at the moment of fission.

When Fermi heard the news about nuclear fission, he realized that he had split the atom himself five years ago, but had not known it! Many years later, Fermi and some other scientists were looking at an architect's sketches for a new laboratory to be built at the University of Chicago. The sketches showed a vague outline of a human figure, which was to be part of a sculpture over the entrance, and the scientists were guessing what the figure was supposed to represent. Fermi commented dryly that it was probably a scientist *not* discovering fission!

In 1939, Fermi did not waste any time in self-criticism. Here was a magnificent new frontier to explore: How could the atom's great power be controlled? How could it be put to work? He immediately went to work on these questions, and the key to the solution he found was the neutron. This, in his own words, is how Fermi reasoned about nuclear fission:

The neutron enters and causes an instability in the uranium nucleus and it's split apart. A great deal of energy is released. . . . But the circumstances are those in which, in all probability, neutrons will be emitted as well, and this is at the root of the matter. For if the neutrons are emitted in greater number than they are absorbed, a chain reaction will be possible and the way to a new source of energy will have been found.

If, as Fermi hoped, the fission of one atom of uranium produced two neutrons, these might collide with two more atoms of uranium and cause them to emit two neutrons each. Now there would be four neutrons, which would split four atoms, and so forth. This would be a self-sustaining chain reaction. As Fermi put it, in the succinct style which is characteristic of him:

If an original fission causes more than one subsequent fission, then of course the reaction goes. If an original fission causes less than one subsequent fission, then the reaction does not go.

Fermi's prediction that neutrons would be produced in uranium fission was verified two months after he made it. Now it was time to step out of the role of theoretician and enter the laboratory; and this is what Fermi did. He found a laboratory at Columbia and a team: Leo Szilard, a Hungarian-born refugee, Herbert

Anderson, and Walter Zinn. But Fermi could not begin to build his chain-reacting machine, as he called it, until some major problems were solved.

One problem was uranium. Only 0.7 per cent of uranium is fissionable; this minute percentage is known as U-235. Logically, the best way to produce a chain reaction was to separate U-235 from the rest of uranium and use it exclusively. This, however, was a vastly expensive and time-consuming process. Scientists were not even sure it *could* be done.

Fermi, who knew more about how neutrons behave than anyone else, thought that he could produce a chain reaction in ordinary, unseparated uranium. But in 1939 uranium was scarce. Only a few grams of it were available, and these were in labs scattered around the country. Also, very little was known about the properties of uranium. It had to be tested and studied, as well as procured in quantity, before work could proceed.

But these were not the only problems. Fermi and Szilard discovered that the neutrons produced in uranium fission moved too fast to hit the important U-235 atoms; a slow-moving neutron would have a better chance. Fermi was familiar with this problem; he had once used a goldfish pond to slow down neutrons. Now he experimented further and proved that carbon atoms were the most effective of the available slowing-down agents. The carbon, however, had to be very pure, and, unfortunately, a pure form of graphite (which is carbon in a dense, solid form) was just as hard to find as uranium.

After some months of research, Fermi was able to visualize his chain-reacting machine. It would be made of alternating layers of graphite bricks and lumps of uranium embedded in graphite; in other words, it would be a pile. The fast-moving neutrons produced by fissioning U-235 would collide with carbon atoms, slow down, and then hit more U-235 atoms. A chain of fissions would build up; energy would multiply at a furious, but foreseeable, rate.

Fermi's pile could exist only in his imagination, however, unless money could be found to develop several tons of pure graphite and uranium. Therefore he and his co-workers decided to go to the government for funds.

Fermi had another, a far more pressing, reason to tell the United States authorities about his work. In 1939, when Hitler had already begun to blitzkrieg Europe, it was clear to Fermi, who had had some experience with a dictatorship, that a war with Germany was inevitable. He knew that there were physicists in Germany who were working on uranium fission. If Hitler was backing them, Germany might soon have nuclear power for battleships and bombs.

Fermi was not the only physicist who was worrying about war. In the winter of 1939 Leo Szilard had come to Fermi and asked him not to publish anything about his work that might help German scientists.

Fermi had not liked this idea at first. He had seen all too much of censorship in Italy and believed firmly in a free exchange of ideas between scientists. He soon saw that Szilard was right, however, and agreed to censor himself, as did other scientists, here and abroad, who were working on nuclear fission.

But self-censorship was not enough. The United States authorities had to be alerted to the potentialities of the work now going on at Columbia University. Fermi knew that the Navy wanted battleships with an unlimited cruising range. He thought his pile could be used for this purpose (as it was, years later, in the *Nautilus*), as well as for research on explosives, so he went to see the Navy.

His visit was not a success: the Navy took no action. This is not particularly surprising, because at that time a controlled chain reaction was just a theoretical possibility, a bare possibility. Scientists had no proof that it could be done.

But the bare possibility continued to bother the men who would someday have to take the responsibility for unleashing the atom's power. When Hitler stopped the sale of Czechoslovakian uranium and it looked as if Germany was in an all-out effort to get atomic power, the scientists acted again. This time their representatives, Leo Szilard, Eugene Wigner, and Edward Teller, went to Einstein. His warnings, they felt, would be heeded.

When they told Einstein how close to a chain re-action their studies had taken them, he agreed to send his now-famous letter to President Roosevelt, telling him of American and German work on nuclear fission and warning him that "it may be possible to set up a nuclear chain reaction . . . and it is conceivable, though much less certain, that extremely powerful bombs of a new type may thus be constructed."

The scientists who felt their responsibility so keenly and who saw to it that the United States govern-ment was alerted were all refugees from Europe. To-ward the end of the Second World War, Winston Churchill, in a speech, thanked Hitler and Mussolini for sending the Allies Enrico Fermi and the other refugee-scientists!

Soon after Roosevelt received Einstein's letter, he appointed an Advisory Committee on Uranium (Fermi was chairman of the section on Theoretical Aspects), and the small amount of six thousand dollars was ap-propriated for research. Six thousand dollars would not procure much graphite and uranium of the required purity, and therefore research on the pile progressed slowly.

Fermi, Szilard, and Wigner continued to worry. They knew that German physicists were as capable and probably as well informed as themselves. They knew that the United States must work fast to beat Germany to a nuclear weapon. But these scientists from Europe were not accustomed to dealing with government officials. They could not get their ideas across; they could not communicate the urgency they felt.

This situation changed dramatically when, on December 6, 1941, the day before Pearl Harbor, the government announced an all-out drive to develop atomic energy. The next day the United States entered World War II. Then, as Mrs. Fermi put it, "at the same moment Enrico found himself doing war work and became an enemy alien."

The Fermis could not become American citizens until they had lived in America for five years (they became citizens in 1944). Meanwhile Enrico Fermi, as the national of an enemy country, had to obey certain regulations. One of them was that he could not travel unless he first obtained a special permit for each trip from a United States attorney.

Now that the United States had decided to back the development of atomic energy, Fermi had to make frequent trips to Chicago, which had been made headquarters for work on the chain reaction, and for each trip he had to have a special permit. Also, he had to go by train, because enemy aliens were forbidden to board a plane. Fermi, who disliked traveling, never complained about the long train rides or about the inconvenience of having to get special government permission for work the government itself had hired him to do.

Some years later the United States government

took steps to protect its enemy-alien employee as well as to protect itself from him. Bodyguards were assigned to Fermi and to some of the other atomic scientists. These guards were young intelligence agents; one of their duties was to see to it that the scientists did not talk about their work where it might be overheard by unfriendly ears. Censoring the scientists, who earlier had voluntarily censored themselves, was not an easy job, as Fermi's guard, John Baudino, discovered.

Baudino made it a point to ask Fermi questions about his work. If Dr. Fermi is kept busy talking about nuclear fission to me, Baudino figured, he will be less likely to talk to other people and reveal secrets. Fermi, who loved nothing better than to teach, responded magnificently to this treatment. Before long John Baudino knew more about nuclear physics than he had ever imagined was possible, and Fermi began to refer to his guard as "my colleague" when he introduced him to friends. "Soon Baudino will have to have a bodyguard too!" Fermi commented.

In spite of committee meetings and long train rides, Fermi's work progressed. By the summer of 1941 he had enough graphite and uranium, and knew enough about them, to build an experimental pile. This was not intended to produce a chain reaction but only to see whether one was possible. The number of neutrons that would be absorbed by uranium and graphite and thus lost to the chain reaction was still unknown. Also unknown was the degree to which impurities in the pile and leakage would steal neutrons from the reaction. Would enough neutrons be produced within the pile to offset these losses? This question was crucial. The answer to it, which was arrived at only after complex and lengthy figuring, was an estimate that fluctuated, depending on the size and shape of the test pile and the purity of the materials used in it. This estimated number was known as the reproduction factor, or k-factor. Fermi knew that if the k-factor was less than 1, there was no chance of ever producing a chain reaction. If it was more than 1, the chances were better.

The first experimental pile was a disappointment. Its k-factor was less than 1: more neutrons were escaping from the pile or being absorbed within it than were colliding with U-235 atoms. It was necessary that the graphite and uranium be more refined, and more of both were needed so that a larger pile could be built.

Before long the k-factor would become one of the top secrets of World War II, but at this time few men outside Fermi's team were worrying about it. An atomic pile was only one approach to the problem of getting a chain reaction, and even if the pile worked, it would not itself produce the kind of power needed for a bomb. A far more promising approach was the separation of U-235 from uranium, and government-backed scientists were working hard on this. Then an important discovery changed the whole picture.

The element Fermi had sought seven years before,

when he first bombarded uranium—element 93—was discovered. This element is very unstable, disintegrating rapidly to form element 94, plutonium. Scientists had predicted, even before plutonium was discovered, that it would be as explosive as U-235 and therefore a potential bomb material. The important question was: Can plutonium be produced faster than U-235? The answer was, Yes, if Fermi's pile works! For if the pile worked, it could be used to produce plutonium, and the plutonium could easily be extracted from it by chemical means.

Now government interest focused on Fermi's work, and graphite and uranium began to pour into the laboratory at Columbia University. Before long, one of the experimental piles had reached the ceiling. A larger room was needed and there was none to be had at Columbia.

Herbert Anderson was scouting around New York, looking for a loft, when word arrived that the whole project would be moved to Chicago. Arthur Compton, who was in charge of the government's program to obtain plutonium, wanted to concentrate all the work in one location.

Graphite, uranium, and Geiger counters were packed up and shipped to the University of Chicago, addressed to the "Metallurgical Laboratory," which was the code name for the pile project. Fermi's team was assigned to the squash courts under the west stands of Stagg Field, the only space left on the campus that was large enough. They went to work immediately, and soon the floor was black and greasy with graphite dust. It was as slippery as a dance floor.

The atmosphere in the squash court was tense; the work was speeded up. Fermi played a vigorous part in every aspect of it. No task was too dirty or too tiresome for him if it furthered the project. He soldered pieces of laboratory equipment when it was necessary or carried graphite blocks to a bench saw and pushed them through as they disappeared in clouds of black dust.

Fermi was qualified in more ways than one to direct the speeded-up project at Chicago. He had always been interested in saving time, in eliminating unnecessary steps and unnecessary details. Most of his laboratory constructions were very crude. He did not care how they looked; if they worked, that was the important thing. Never build more elaborately or measure with more care than the task requires—this was his philosophy.

At first Fermi and his team built more test piles in the squash court. When each new batch of uranium and graphite arrived, a small pile was made to test their purity or, in other words, to discover their k-factor. This figure could only be obtained after a series of complex mathematical operations, and Fermi insisted on always doing these himself, because he knew that he could get the correct answer in the shortest time. The men on Fermi's team always could tell whether or not he was in his office. If they did not hear the noise of the calculating machine on his desk, they did not bother to knock, but looked for him in the nearest laboratory.

In June, 1942, one of the test piles finally showed a k-factor of more than 1. At last work could begin on the real thing. A huge structure of graphite and uranium began to take shape in the squash court under Stagg Field. There were two construction crews working on it, one under Anderson, the other under Zinn. They labored almost around the clock.

Fermi and his men had calculated that the most effective shape for the pile was a sphere. This would be supported by a square wooden frame. There was no need to build a neutron source into the pile to start the chain reaction. Neutrons from the spontaneous fission of uranium and from other sources would start the reaction automatically when the pile reached the critical size.

But what was the critical size? The scientists could only guess at that. There were too many unknowns, too many variables. All they knew for sure was that the pile had to be as big as possible, as big as the room would permit. The larger the pile, the fewer the chances that neutrons would escape into the air before they bombarded uranium atoms.

For a long time Fermi was not sure that a chain reaction would be achieved. Perhaps the pile would reach the ceiling of the squash court before it went critical. What could be done about this? he wondered.

He knew that if the air could be removed from the pile, it would help, because air absorbs neutrons. Then Fermi thought of canning the pile, enclosing it in some kind of container so that, if necessary, the air could be pumped out. That was why the Goodyear Tire and Rubber Company received an order for a huge square balloon, dimensioned to fit over the pile, wooden frame and all. The Goodyear people, of course, did not know what the balloon was for, and they were worried. They doubted that it would fly!

When the balloon arrived at the squash court, Fermi had himself hoisted up near the ceiling, where he could direct operations as the balloon was fitted over the pile. When he called out to haul on a rope here, brace a tackle there, and heave, he looked to the men below like an admiral on a bridge. So for a while Fermi was known as "Admiral" around the labs.

As the scientists laid layer after layer of graphite and uranium, they kept a close watch on the instruments that recorded radioactivity. Because it was possible to reach the critical size at any time, thus setting off a chain reaction, there had to be a control device built into the pile. This was a series of neutron-absorbing rods, made of cadmium. When the rods were in place, a chain reaction was impossible. When they were drawn out, the scientists could measure just how critical the pile was getting to be.

Late in the evening of December 1, 1942, almost four years after Fermi began to work on the problem of a chain reaction, tests showed that the pile had reached the critical size. This happened somewhat earlier than the scientists had estimated (the square balloon was not necessary after all), and so the sphere never was completed. Instead of a ball, it looked rather like a doorknob.

On the morning of December 2, Fermi reported to the squash court at eight-thirty, as usual. This was the day that would tell the story. The scientists who had worked on the pile gathered around it. Now their decisions and calculations would be given a final test. Few of them knew that the United States government had already made arrangements for three huge plutonium-producing piles, patterned after the one in the squash court. Three hundred and fifty million dollars had been bet on the success of their work.

Fermi climbed to a balcony at one end of the squash court from which he could direct his men. There were three sets of control rods in the pile. One set was controlled automatically. Another was an emergency rod, which would be operated by Walter Zinn. It was named "Zip" and was a precaution in case, once begun, the chain reaction got out of control and the automatic rods failed to drop into place. The third and last rod would be drawn out slowly by a young physicist named George Weil.

According to calculations, any one of the control rods could prevent a chain reaction. But the unexpected might happen and so the "suicide squad" was ready: three young men on a platform above the pile, ready to flood it with a solution of cadmium if the chain reaction got out of control.

First Fermi rehearsed each man in his part. Then the automatic control rods were removed.

At 9:45 A.M. Fermi called, "Zip out." Walter Zinn drew out the rod by hand and tied it to a rail of the balcony. Now there was only one rod left in the pile. George Weil stood beside it, ready to operate it when Fermi gave him the word.

On the balcony there were counters and other instruments. One of these was a recorder, whose quivering pen would trace an upward line, indicating the intensity of radiation within the pile. If everything happened according to plan, this line would move upward and then level off as, foot by foot, the last rod was drawn out. When the rod was all the way out, and the chain reaction began, the line would continue upward and not level off.

"Now we shall see if our calculations are correct," said Fermi to some visitors. It was clear to everyone that Fermi himself was sure that they *were* correct. One person who was present described him as being "completely self-confident but wholly without conceit." He remained cool and deliberate during a day that aroused very different feelings in the other participants.

Now Fermi, his eyes fixed on the instruments, called out, "Pull it to thirteen feet, George." Turning to the onlookers, he indicated the recorder. "The pen will move upward to this point and then level off," he told them.

No one spoke as the rod was pulled out, the counters began to click, and the pen traveled upward. It leveled off at exactly the point Fermi had indicated. Again Fermi asked Weil to pull the rod out, a little further this time. Again the pen reached the point Fermi had calculated and then leveled off. As this series of events was repeated over and over, the visitors, fascinated, watched the pen of the recorder and the pile below "obey" Fermi. Before they realized it, it was midday. Fermi had not yet given the order to remove the entire rod. It was wiser to proceed cautiously, step by step. Tension in the room was growing.

"I'm hungry," Fermi announced, to everyone's surprise. "Let's go to lunch."

After lunch everyone took his place and the experiment continued. Foot by foot, the rod was drawn out. Finally, at 3:25 in the afternoon, Fermi told George Weil to pull the rod another foot out of the pile, the last foot. Fermi turned to Arthur Compton, who was standing at his side. "This is going to do it," he told Compton.

Weil removed the last rod from the pile. The pen climbed upward without leveling off. Soon the Geiger counters were recording so fast that their click-clicks could not be distinguished by the human ear.

Fermi reached for his slide rule and began to compute the rate at which neutrons were being produced.

A minute later, and again three minutes after that, he repeated this computation. If the rate remained constant, he would know that the chain reaction was self-sustaining.

Later George Weil described this moment. "I had to watch Fermi every second, waiting for orders. His face was motionless. His eyes darted from one dial to another. His expression was so calm it was hard. But suddenly, his whole face broke into a broad smile."

Fermi closed his slide rule. "The reaction is self-sustaining," he announced.

He allowed the pile to operate for twenty-eight minutes. Then, "Zip in," he called; and the experiment was over. For the first time, man had created a self-sustaining chain reaction and then controlled it.

Eugene Wigner produced a bottle of red wine. The scientists solemnly drank it from paper cups, then signed the straw-covered wine bottle. No one suggested a toast. They could have drunk to the dawn of the atomic age. Most scientists agree that December 2, 1942, is the date it began.

In the summer of 1942 the War Department's Corps of Engineers had taken over the Plutonium Project, giving it the code name "Manhattan District." The Army wanted plutonium for bombs. They wanted it in quantity and they wanted it fast. For the next two years Fermi worked as designer, engineer, and consultant as immense atomic piles went into production, first at Oak Ridge, Tennessee; then at Hanford, Washington.

The original Chicago pile was disassembled and moved to a new location outside the city, at Argonne National Laboratory. There it was rebuilt and Fermi used it both as a pilot plant for larger, more complex piles and as a tool for fundamental research in nuclear physics.

One of the first problems that had to be solved before the government's atomic piles could go into production was shielding. There had to be protection against the enormous amounts of radiation that would be produced. What should these shields be made of? How thick must they be?

Fermi proposed to get the answers by experimenting with the original pile. He calculated that steel and paraffin were the best materials for the job and then had sample compositions of these materials prepared. These samples were placed near the top of the pile, and for two weeks Fermi measured furiously for he was working against time. He was only able to get incomplete answers and since there was no time to experiment further, he had to rely on his intuition and mathematical skill. In spite of this, he found solutions to the problem, and the solutions were correct. They were still being used in 1955.

The instinct that enabled Fermi to take short cuts to reach a solution saved the Army much time in its all-out drive for bomb material. This was demonstrated rather dramatically at Hanford, Washington, in 1944. A huge plutonium pile there was just going into production. It had reached the critical point, the control rods were all the way out, when the pile stopped. The operators were nonplused; Fermi was called in. With the help of his slide rule, he was able to diagnose the trouble in a very short time. One of the products of fission, an isotope of xenon, was absorbing neutrons at an enormous rate. It was not hard to find a cure for this condition once the cause was identified.

Fermi was famous, even among scientists, for the things he could do with his slide rule. S. K. Allison has described a train ride he once took with Arthur Compton and Fermi. They were going out to Washington, to visit the Hanford plant, and the trip was long. Fermi seemed bored and Arthur Compton decided to give him something to do.

"When I was studying cosmic rays in the Andes Mountains," he told Fermi, "I observed that my watch did not keep good time at high altitudes." Dr. Compton went on to say that he had thought about this a great deal since and had finally found a satisfactory explanation. What did Fermi think it was?

Fermi came to attention. His eyes flashed at the delightful prospect of a problem to solve. He reached for his slide rule and found some paper. For five minutes he was busy with equations for the entrainment of air in the balance wheel of the watch, the effect on the period of the wheel, and the change in this effect at the low pressures of high altitudes. Then he told Arthur Compton exactly what kind of time his watch had kept in the Andes.

S. K. Allison, who had been watching the two scientists, has said that he is not likely to forget the look on Dr. Compton's face when Fermi came up with the right answer.

Enrico Fermi had played a decisive part in the research and development that made an atomic bomb possible. His next job, one might expect, would have to do with the design of the weapon itself. It did. In 1944 Fermi went to Los Alamos, New Mexico, where he was in charge of the division for advanced development of the A-bomb.

Los Alamos was a hotbed of theoretical physicists because the bomb, of necessity, was a product of calculation. In essence the bomb was an *uncontrolled* chain reaction; there could be no cadmium rods to slow it down or stop it. Therefore scientists could not pile up fissionable material until a critical size was reached; they had to calculate the critical size. And if they calculated wrong, there would be no explosion—or no Los Alamos.

As consultant on all phases of the bomb's design, Fermi kept his slide rule in constant use. When a scientist came to him with some interesting experimental results, Fermi would not look at them. "Just tell me what you set out to do in the experiment," he would say, "and then I will calculate the final result. If my calculation checks with your experiment, we can be quite sure that the results obtained are correct."

This approach was characteristic of Enrico Fermi.

He would not accept experimental results at their face value, but always tried to find out how they had been obtained. When he saw a report of an experiment in a scientific journal, he would read only until the problem to be solved was fully set forth. Then he would use his slide rule to calculate the solution for himself and see how it checked. This took him less time than reading how the author had proceeded to get the answers.

Though the pressure to get an A-bomb was great, Fermi was able to get away from the laboratory once in a while to ski or climb the mountains near Los Alamos. Emilio Segré, his old friend and collaborator from Rome, was also working on the bomb, and they often skied together. Fermi went at this with great enthusiasm but not much style, crouching as low as possible on his skis to avoid falls. Like his laboratory constructions, his skiing was serviceable but crude. It got him down the hill in a hurry, though, and he delighted in tiring out younger men on these expeditions. One day, so the story goes, Fermi and his bodyguard, John Baudino, returned from the slopes with Baudino in such a state of exhaustion that Fermi was carrying his gun!

Fermi's work at Los Alamos came to a violent conclusion on July 16, 1945. On that day, at Alamogordo, the first atomic bomb was exploded. The men who had made it looked on. They and many others have described the explosion: the intensity of light, the violence of the air blast, the deafening roar.

Possibly Fermi was the only witness who did not

hear the bomb explode. He was busily dropping pieces of paper to the ground when it went off and said later that he had heard nothing. The air blast made by the bomb blew the paper quite a distance, and Fermi paced this off, counting his steps. From this figure he was able to calculate the power of the blast. His simple experiment gave him the same figure obtained by the complex instruments that had been set up for the same purpose.

After Fermi finished his calculations, he climbed into a lead-lined Sherman tank and explored the crater left by the first nuclear weapon ever to be exploded.

The final decision to drop the atomic bomb on Japanese cities was President Truman's. Before making it, he appointed an advisory committee, and one of the four scientists who consulted with this committee was Enrico Fermi. The committee advised the President to use the bomb.

Many of the atomic scientists felt responsible for the bomb's destruction of Hiroshima and Nagasaki. Some of them believed that they should have stopped work when they first realized that an atomic bomb was possible. Fermi did not agree with this. Ignorance can never be better than knowledge, he thought, even if knowledge is painful.

In 1949, however, when a "super-" or H-bomb became a possibility, Fermi went on record as follows:

The fact that no limits exist to the destructiveness of this weapon [the H-bomb] makes its very existence and the knowledge of its construction a danger to humanity as a

whole. It is necessarily an evil thing considered in any light.
. . . It [is] important for the President of the United States
to tell the American public and the world that we think
it wrong on fundamental ethical principles to initiate the
development of such a weapon.

Even the scientists who disagreed completely with
Fermi's political opinions had respect for them. This
was because he was careful to think out his views as
much as possible and tried to avoid prejudice in all
things. He was objective about his own abilities, too.
Fermi knew perfectly well that he had an exceptional
mind, had no false modesty about it, and was quite willing to accept praise when it was due. He was not a self-
effacing man.

He could not apply his rational approach to everything, of course. When it was a matter of art, Fermi
was at a loss. "It seems incredible to me," he told one
of his students, "that someone would want to paint sky
green or a meadow blue." He also admitted that music
meant very little to him. He only liked the simplest
tunes.

One day at Los Alamos, after most of the work on
the bomb had been completed, Fermi and Segré were
talking about their plans for the future. Fermi was then
forty-four years old. Few physicists have done important
creative work after forty, so now would be the time for
Fermi to retire and work on refinements of his past discoveries. He could become "king of the neutrons," as
Segré put it.

This idea did not appeal to Fermi at all. He laughed and quoted one of Mussolini's slogans: *"Rinnovarsi o perire,"* "to renew oneself or to perish." Before long he was hard at work, exploring other new frontiers in physics.

Fermi returned to the University of Chicago in 1946. He had accepted an honorary professorship and was also a member of the new Institute of Nuclear Physics, a foundation for basic research. At the Institute Fermi played with a fascinating new gadget, a cyclotron, which he had helped design. By means of the cyclotron's radio-frequency field, particles were accelerated to enormous speeds and then used to break up atomic nuclei. With the help of the cyclotron, Fermi studied mesons, particles that are associated with the force that holds the nucleus—and therefore all matter —together.

During this period he also became interested in the fast-moving particles from space called cosmic rays and came up with a theory to explain their origin. This theory postulated the existence in outer space of enormous magnetic fields which, like the cyclotron but on a far larger scale, could accelerate particles. Recent astronomical observations support Fermi's theory.

His cosmic-ray theory is another instance of the great span of Fermi's contributions to physics, a span that is particularly striking today, when it has become difficult for a scientist to keep up with all the developments in his own specialty, much less his entire science.

Hans Bethe, himself a celebrated physicist, has said that "Fermi may have been one of the last physicists who knew almost all of physics and used it in his research."

In spite of a schedule crowded with classes and research, Fermi always found time for exercise, which he still believed should be taken systematically. He rode his bike to class every day and was always trying to tire out his students on long hikes, or swims in Lake Michigan. One student remembers him at a party, where children's games were being played for the fun of it. There Fermi got into a penny-pitching game, but he got right out of it again when he found that he was not good enough at it to win. At the same party he was also seen trying, with complete absorption, to win a game of musical chairs.

Fermi was apt to choose young people for friends and his physics classes were jammed with students. This was not because he applied a sweet icing of jokes to the subject matter. On the contrary, he was intensely serious when he taught physics. He was sure that he could explain anything, no matter how difficult, so that his students could understand it. This involvement with his subject, and delight in making it understandable to others, was infectious. Many students who took his courses decided to become physicists and, in this way, his influence will be felt for a long time.

Enrico Fermi died of cancer on September 29, 1954. He knew before he died that his condition would be fatal and those who saw him at that time have said that he tried hard to put them at their ease. They say, too, that his last summer, which he spent in southern France and Italy, was a happy one on the whole. One acquaintance remembers an argument between Fermi and some friends who were visiting him that summer. Certain members of the party wanted to take a car on an excursion through the Italian countryside. Fermi was vehemently opposed to this. He, of course, wanted to go on foot.

If Fermi had lived longer, he would have seen his own creation, the atomic pile, used to save lives. In 1959 the first pile designed for medical use exclusively was completed. It is located at Brookhaven National Laboratory, in New York, and among its many uses will be the treatment of brain cancer patients.

It is sad, too, that Fermi did not live to see the atomic pile at Shippingport, Pennsylvania, which went critical in 1957. This is the first full-scale pile in the United States to supply power for living: for electric lights, stoves, and the automatic labor-saving gadgets that fascinated Fermi and which he thought were symbolic of America.

Enrico Fermi was honored in many ways both before and after his death. He was given the Congressional Medal of Merit in 1946; and the Atomic Energy Commission, which awarded him $25,000 in 1954, announced that their future awards to scientists would be named after him. Fermi's name has also been perpetuated by The Institute of Nuclear Physics, which is now

The Enrico Fermi Institute, and by the designation of a new element—Fermium 100.

Fermi's friends and fellow-scientists have paid him many tributes as teacher, as administrator, as scientist, as man. Perhaps none of these tributes is as eloquent as the words spoken by Arthur Compton on the day Fermi's pile went critical and produced the first controlled nuclear energy.

Professor Compton had called Dr. James Conant at Harvard to tell him the news. Anything about atomic energy was top secret at the time, and so Compton had to improvise a code. When he got Dr. Conant on the line, Arthur Compton announced the news in words that were immediately understood:

"The Italian navigator has reached the New World."

CHAPTER 18

Jonas E. Salk

During the spring and summer of 1954 a million and a half American school children took part in a major scientific experiment. Some of these boys and girls were given shots of a cherry-colored vaccine which, it was hoped, would protect them against polio, or infantile paralysis, as it is often called.

Other children, acting as a scientific control, were inoculated with a useless fluid, called a placebo. This also was cherry-colored. The child who was given a shot did not know whether he was getting vaccine or placebo. Neither did his parents know, or even the doctor who gave the shot. Only the scientists in charge of the experiment could tell, from code numbers on each vial that was used, whether it had contained vaccine or placebo. Thus the experiment was planned so that the opinions and feelings of those involved could not affect the results.

Careful records were kept to see how many children in each of the two groups caught polio during the epidemic season that followed, and what variety of polio it was. These facts and figures were compared with similar statistics for past polio epidemics and then, eleven months after the experiment had begun, the results were announced: a polio vaccine had been found that was safe and that worked. It had protected from paralytic polio an average of 79 per cent of the children who had received it.

A grave problem faced the board of scientists who met together directly after the announcement was made. It was up to them to decide whether the new vaccine should be licensed by the United States government and thus approved for immediate mass production and mass use.

One ingredient of the vaccine, a virus known as the "Mahoney strain," was the cause of a deadly form of polio. Although the Mahoney strain had been "cooked" in a solution of formaldehyde designed to kill each tiny, lethal virus, tests had revealed that in some lots of vaccine, viruses still survived. These lots had never been used on human beings and rigorous laboratory and testing methods had been worked out to insure a safe vaccine. Nevertheless the more conservative scientists on the board felt that children throughout the United

States should not be given the vaccine until it had been tested and improved over a longer period of time.

Other scientists felt that such a delay could not be justified. Between thirty-five and fifty thousand people would become infected by polio during the coming year. Should the board of scientists withhold protection from these thousands who, according to statistics, would die or become paralyzed?

A majority of the scientists on the board believed that the vaccine should be put on the market right away. While it was being used to save lives, it could be studied and improved. Therefore the anti-polio vaccine was licensed and the rest is history.

An intensive search for an effective vaccine against polio began in the late 1930's. This search was in some ways like a war, a war of many campaigns, each led by a different general. At the head of one of the final campaigns was Jonas Salk, a quiet, intense young doctor who, to his dismay, became one of the most publicized scientists of his time.

Jonas Edward Salk was born in New York City on October 28, 1914, two years before the worst polio epidemic ever reported spread through the United States. His father, Daniel Salk, was a manufacturer of women's clothes, or "women's wear" as it is called in the fiercely competitive garment district of New York; and the Salk family was never well-to-do. To help pay for his education, Jonas, the eldest of the three boys in the family, took part-time jobs and in the summer worked as a counselor in a boys' camp.

Jonas was an intelligent boy. He read widely and studied hard; but he showed no particular interest in science. Physics was the only science course he took while he was at Townsend Harris Hall, a high school for accelerated students. Then, during his freshman year at the College of the City of New York, he decided to take a few science courses "out of curiosity," as he puts it. He became so interested in them that he gave up his intention to become a lawyer and began to study science in earnest. His logical mind and neat, precise way of going about things fitted him well for research.

When Jonas finished college (he was then only nineteen), he decided to study medicine, not in order to practice it but to prepare for a career in medical research. Several people advised him that he would never make much money in research, but this did not matter at all to Jonas. He did not think that having money was important. Years later when he became famous and was besieged with invitations to speak, to sponsor causes, and even to endorse products, he turned these offers down, though they would have paid him well. "Most of this belongs in the category of mink coats and Cadillacs—unnecessary," was his comment.

While Jonas was in New York University Medical School, he won a fellowship to do research in protein chemistry. Then, in his fourth year, he began to study viruses, working under Dr. Thomas Francis, Jr., a noted virus specialist who played an important part in Jonas's later career.

Viruses had been discovered only forty-four years before, by a Russian scientist named Ivanovski. He did not actually see these infinitesimal dots (one million polio viruses in a row would barely measure an inch) but deduced their existence from various experiments. Further research by other scientists revealed that viruses had a unique and dangerous characteristic. Unlike bacteria, which are self-sufficient, viruses can reproduce themselves only after they enter the living cells of the individual they attack. After a virus enters a cell, it takes over the cell's processes, uses them to produce more viruses, and in so doing, usually damages or destroys the cell.

The viruses that cause paralytic polio are likely to single out nerve cells for attack. That is the reason for the name "poliomyelitis," which is derived from the Greek words for "gray marrow" and means an inflammation of the gray matter inside the spine.

Polio is not a recent disease; traces of it have even been found in Egyptian mummies. Yet before the twentieth century there are almost no records of polio epidemics; and the reason for this, oddly enough, is sanitation. Polio viruses are found in human excrement and in the past these wastes were not conveniently flushed away. Therefore most people were exposed to mild forms of polio at any early age, so that they built up a resistance to the disease. As the sanitary disposal of human wastes became more and more widespread, people were less and and less likely to be exposed to polio while they were young. And the older a person is when first exposed, the more intense is the polio infection that develops.

Although as sanitation improved, polio became more and more of a menace, until quite recently scientists knew very little about it. Polio research was slowed down by a lack of over-all planning and funds. What was needed was an organization, backed by a large sum of money, that would pay for simultaneous research on many different aspects of polio. This much-needed organization, for the treatment of patients as well as for research, was established in 1938 by a famous polio victim, President Franklin D. Roosevelt. It was named the National Foundation for Infantile Paralysis and was supported by a March of Dimes, contributed by the American people.

A year after the National Foundation was set up, Jonas Salk received his M.D. Thus Salk's education was almost complete just at the time a full-scale investigation of polio got under way. It was not long before he joined the ranks of scientists who were working with the Foundation.

These scientists were trying to make an anti-polio vaccine. In order to do this, they had to find a safe way to inject polio viruses into the human body. In response to this safe virus attack, the human system would produce polio antibodies, substances that fight off the disease. And a person who had this antibody defense in his blood would be immune to polio.

Three huge factors blocked the way to the development of an anti-polio vaccine. First, scientists had to have a plentiful supply of polio viruses to experiment with, so that they could learn something about them. But until 1949 they knew only one way to grow viruses. They would inoculate a monkey with a small quantity of viruses and wait until he became infected and the viruses multiplied within his nervous system. Then the monkey would be killed and his spinal cord, which contained the viruses, removed. This method was slow, expensive (a monkey cost about thirty dollars), and—most important—dangerous. Viruses grown in this way could not be injected into the human body, because they might cause an allergic inflammation of the brain, a condition deadlier than polio itself.

In one stroke, a research team headed by John F. Enders solved this double problem. They demonstrated a way to grow viruses in test tubes, so that they could be produced in volume; and they grew the viruses in safe, non-nervous tissue.

That was one problem out of the way; two remained. There was reason to think that when polio viruses attacked an individual, they traveled by nerve pathways and never entered the bloodstream. If this was the case, a vaccine would be useless, because no matter how many antibodies were produced in the bloodstream, they would never encounter the virus enemy. In 1952, two scientists, working independently, solved this problem. They discovered that in the very early stages of polio infection, which had not been thoroughly investigated before, viruses did circulate in the bloodstream. Dorothy Horstmann and David Bodian's discovery meant that polio could be fought with a vaccine.

The third problem, simple to state but difficult to answer, was: How many types of polio are there? A vaccine would be useful only if it protected against all types of polio, and scientists had collected specimens of as many as one hundred different polio viruses. These specimens would have to be tested, compared, and classified—a gigantic job. The National Foundation for Infantile Paralysis commissioned four university laboratories to handle the project.

At the head of one of these laboratories was Jonas Salk. After interning at Mount Sinai Hospital, in New York City, Dr. Salk had won a National Research Council fellowship. This had enabled him to go to the University of Michigan's School of Public Health, which was headed by his former medical school professor, Thomas Francis, Jr.

Since medical school, Jonas Salk had grown more and more interested in preventive medicine, interested specifically in the development of vaccines that would protect people from virus epidemics. "As a medical scientist," he said, "I've had training and opportunities beyond those of many other people. I feel an obligation to use them for socially useful ends."

The first enemy to society that Dr. Salk took on was the influenza virus. Together, Dr. Salk and Dr. Francis studied influenza, seeking more effective ways to immunize against it. When, in 1947, Salk left the University of Michigan to head a virus research laboratory of his own at the University of Pittsburgh, he continued to study influenza and was hard at work on the immunization problems it presented when the National Foundation asked him to take part in their polio-typing project. He agreed to take on the new task partly out of curiosity, and soon was absorbed in the delicate, precise work of typing different virus strains.

Before the job was completed, in 1951, Dr. Salk's laboratory and the three others that were working on the project used thirty thousand monkeys and spent more than a million dollars. The conclusion they reached was encouraging: the one hundred different virus strains fell into three broad classifications, or types (called simply Type I, Type II, and Type III). This meant that a vaccine containing only the three virus types could give protection against all varieties of polio.

By the time Dr. Salk had completed his part of the typing job, he understood the steps that would have to be taken to make an anti-polio vaccine. Although he had studied polio only a short time in comparison with other scientists in the field, this, some people feel, may have been an asset. Because the problems presented by polio were new to him, he had few preconceptions about them; his approach was fresh. He also had the ability to organize and schedule numerous procedures, tests, and problems to be solved into a laboratory work program. In short, he was a good administrator.

In the fall of 1951, Jonas Salk was ready to go to work on a vaccine and put the achievements of many different scientists to practical use. Backed by funds from the National Foundation, Salk and the men and women in his Pittsburgh laboratory, who have been called "one of the fastest-working laboratory teams in recent memory," began to make a vaccine.

In essence, with all the fine points, the repeated tests, the trials and errors left out, this is the way the vaccine was prepared: Kidney tissue from rhesus monkeys was minced into tiny pieces and each piece was placed in a bottle. Then, to keep the tissue alive, a feeding solution was added. This solution, called Mixture 199, contained sixty-two ingredients, among them vitamins, minerals, and penicillin.

After the bottles spent a week in an incubator, representative strains of the three polio-virus types (Salk used the Mahoney Strain for Type I) were placed in the bottles, one type to a bottle. Virus particles attached themselves to the kidney cells and began to reproduce, just as they would have in the body of a person who was not protected by polio antibodies.

The next step was to remove the viruses, which

had multiplied many times, from the bottles and test them on small animals to make sure that the viruses were potent and free from contamination. The virus lots that passed these tests were then killed. This was done by submerging them in a chemical bath of formaldehyde, the odorous disinfectant well known to anyone who has dissected animals in a biology class.

Finally, the three types of virus were combined and, after a series of rigorous safety tests, the vaccine—clear and cherry-colored—was ready to be used. Although the polio viruses had been killed by formaldehyde—that is, they had lost the power to infect or multiply—they still had the power to stimulate production of antibodies.

It took Dr. Salk and his laboratory team about a year and a half to develop their anti-polio vaccine. During this time, they were working under pressure, for they knew that the goal was close; but at the same time they had to proceed cautiously, step by step. The full weight of this pressure for both caution and speed fell on Dr. Salk. He spent almost every waking hour in his laboratory, often working sixteen hours a day, six days a week.

Before this hectic period of his life, Dr. Salk had often played tennis and golf. Now he had little free time and this he preferred to spend with his family. In 1939 he had married a dark, slender young woman named Donna Lindsay, who had been a social worker. They had had three sons: Peter, Darrell, and Jonathan.

By the fall of 1952, Jonas Salk's anti-polio vaccine was ready. It had proved to be both safe and effective, but it had been proved only on monkeys. The time had come to test it on children.

First Dr. Salk gave shots to boys and girls who had once had polio and therefore already had antibodies in their blood. When his vaccine caused these children to produce even more antibodies, which is called a "booster effect," and did not harm them in any way, he was ready to inoculate children who had never had polio. His own sons were among the first to receive trial shots.

He observed the same "booster effect," though on a smaller scale, in the children who had had no antibodies in their blood before being given vaccine: when a final shot was given, about seven months after the first series of inoculations, the body responded by producing more antibodies than ever before. It was as if, after a few exposures to polio, the body had learned how to fight off the attack.

As more and more children were inoculated with Salk vaccine, evidence piled up that it was safe and that it triggered the production of polio antibodies. But did it produce *enough* antibodies? When a child who had received vaccine was attacked by live polio viruses, would he be fully protected? There was a simple way to find out: give vaccine to a group of children and then deliberately infect them with polio to see whether or not they fought it off. To risk lives in this way was out of the question.

The alternative was a mass human experiment, or field trial, as it was called, in which thousands of children would be given vaccine and other thousands, the control groups, would not receive vaccine. Then during the epidemic season, both groups would be observed to see how many in each caught polio.

The man in charge of the mass field trial was Jonas Salk's friend and teacher, Thomas Francis, Jr. It was he who planned part of the experiment so that some children received vaccine while others, as a control, received a placebo.

Dr. Francis announced the field trial results to a gathering of scientists, health officials, and reporters. In the jubilation over the news that Salk's vaccine was safe, and was 90 to 100 per cent effective against Type II and Type III polio, another statistic was to some extent overlooked: Against the most dangerous variety of polio, Type I, the vaccine was only 65 per cent effective.

Salk vaccine was licensed immediately for public use, and the laboratories of six large drug companies produced it in large batches, trying to meet the enormous demand for shots. Then, only two weeks after the vaccine had been put on the market, the United States Public Health Service received alarming news. Eleven children who had just been given shots of Salk vaccine had come down with polio. Reports of more cases followed, and in every instance the polio victim had received vaccine made by the same drug company, Cutter Laboratories.

Dr. Salk, shocked and grave, was one of the experts the government called in to find out what had gone wrong and what could be done about it. All vaccine production and all inoculations were stopped until the experts made their report.

There were live viruses in some batches of Cutter Laboratories' vaccine, the experts found. Why had particles of virus escaped death in the formaldehyde solution? The answer was that viruses can form a sediment, or sludge. Within this sediment lie virus particles that are protected from exposure to formaldehyde. They remain in the vaccine, alive and potentially dangerous. Why hadn't tests revealed these live viruses in the vaccine? The answer involves some history.

The drug companies had first begun to produce vaccine at the time of the field trials, because Dr. Salk's laboratory could not supply the large quantity needed. For a while every lot of commercially produced vaccine had been triple-tested for safety, by the drug company that had produced it, by the government, and by Dr. Salk's laboratory. Then the government decided that the drug companies had learned how to make a safe vaccine and that it would be all right "to short-cut a little," as President Eisenhower put it. Therefore the government stopped triple-testing vaccine, and the drug companies did their own testing, except for occasional spot checks, when the Cutter incident occurred.

But, as the Cutter incident showed, the drug companies had not learned how to make a uniformly safe vaccine. For example, it was very important to filter the vaccine, in order to remove virus-containing sediment, shortly before the vaccine was "cooked" in formaldehyde. But some of the drug companies (Cutter Laboratories was not the only one at fault) had allowed too much time to pass between filtering and cooking; and during this time more sediment had formed. Therefore Dr. Salk and the other polio experts on the government's board made detailed rules for vaccine manufacture. Among other things, these rules called for filtering the vaccine both shortly before and during immersion in formaldehyde. The experts also worked out a series of rigorous safety tests, and the Public Health Service went back to double-checking the vaccine. There was no repetition of the Cutter incident—and no possibility of a repetition.

Since improved production techniques and tests were put into effect, there has been no question about the safety of Salk vaccine. However, many authorities believe that it is not as potent or long-lasting as some other anti-polio vaccines, which were developed after Dr. Salk's. These vaccines are made of *live* polio viruses. Although the viruses are alive, they are not dangerous; for they have been bred in laboratories to cause only a mild case of polio, a case so mild that it is unnoticeable. In August, 1960, the Sabin live-virus vaccine was approved by the government for use in the United States.

As the scientist who developed the first safe, effective anti-polio vaccine, Jonas Salk has become a famous man. Millions of people have seen his photograph in newspapers and magazines and have come to know his long face and serious dark eyes behind glasses with colorless rims. He has also been recognized by numerous societies, educational institutions, and by the government of the United States, from whom he has received the Congressional Gold Medal and a Presidential citation. Dr. Salk has received no money from the sale of his vaccine, however. Once he was asked who owned the patent on it and replied, "The people . . . could you patent the sun?"

Perhaps one reason why Jonas Salk is so widely known is that he often left the laboratory to explain his vaccine to the public. He felt personally responsible for what he had made and wanted the public to understand, from his own lips, what the vaccine could and could not do. Therefore he talked to the press and made public appearances and speeches, some of them on television and radio.

Jonas Salk did these things out of a strong sense of social obligation, and not because he wanted fame. But fame is what he got and, unfortunately, this gave him little pleasure. He knew that the work of other scientists had made the vaccine possible; it was embarrassing to be given so much of the credit.

And his fame was not only embarrassing, it was annoying. The time came when it was no longer necessary for him to explain his vaccine to the public, but the demands on his time and attention—from the press, from well-wishers, from people who wanted to capitalize on his name—still continued. Even courteous refusals to these demands took time—time spent away from the research he wanted to do.

In 1958 Dr. Salk was given another March of Dimes grant, and he began work on a vaccine to immunize against all virus diseases of the central nervous system. As part of this research, he made studies of normal and malignant cells, studies that had some bearing on the problems of cancer.

Whether or not his research will bring him another dramatic success in the eyes of the world does not concern Dr. Salk. Someone asked him once, after his vaccine had been proved a success, if he ever felt like a writer who has written a successful first novel and wonders whether he can do it again.

"I don't want to go from one crest to another," Dr. Salk replied. "And science isn't like novel-writing. To a scientist, fame is neither an end nor even a means to an end. Do you recall what Emerson said?—'The reward of a thing well done is the opportunity to do more.'"

CHAPTER 19

Tsung Dao Lee
and Chen Ning Yang

In 1956 two young men broke a law. During the following year the same two young men were given the Nobel
Prize for what they had done.

The two lawbreakers were Tsung Dao Lee and
Chen Ning Yang, physicists. Born in China, they came
to the United States to study when they were just out
of their teens. Ten years later they caused the collapse
of the conservation of parity law, a foundation of the
science of physics.

When they won the Nobel Prize, Lee and Yang
were in their early thirties. (Lee was thirty-one, which
made him the second youngest person ever to win a
Nobel Prize.) Both men are small and lightly built;
their faces are fresh and unwrinkled.

Although the two physicists have a great deal in

common, their personalities are strikingly different. Yang is a sociable person. He is energetic, genial, and quite talkative. During a conversation, his face is very expressive and his slender fingers move in graceful, illustrative gestures. Yang's high forehead, small nose, and full cheeks make him look a bit like a sophisticated cherub; but this impression vanishes when he speaks. He is outspoken and down-to-earth. One feels that he likes to talk to people and would be at ease in most social situations.

Before he left China for the United States, Chen Ning Yang picked out an English first name for himself, because he thought it would be easier for Americans to say than his own name. He had read a biography of Benjamin Franklin and admired him very much, so he chose the name, "Franklin." The friends he made in America soon shortened this to "Frank."

Tsung Dao Lee, on the other hand, did not pick a new name for himself when he came to America— but he soon got one anyway. His acquaintances call him "T. D." For the sake of clarity, from this point on in their biographies the two physicists will be called Frank Yang and T. D. Lee.

The boyish-looking T. D. Lee is sensitive and standoffish. His face is not as expressive as Yang's, but he is decidedly good-looking. Except for strong, heavy eyebrows, his features are as regular and finely delineated as those of a porcelain figurine.

When Lee is asked for his opinion about something that has nothing to do with physics, he is apt not to commit himself. He also does not like to talk much about his personal life, partly because he cannot see why anyone would be interested in it. To a person meeting him for the first time, he gives the impression of a shy boy in a dancing class: a bit restless, a bit out of his element as he tries to cope with the unappealing rhythm of social intercourse. Lee seems suited in every way to be just what he is—a thinker. Yang, on the other hand, could conceivably be, as well as a thinker, a business man or an administrator.

T. D. Lee and Frank Yang were awarded the Nobel Prize in 1957, less than a year after their work had proved the faultiness of the parity law, which made this one of the promptest recognitions in the history of the Nobel awards. In the same year Lee and Yang also received the Albert Einstein Commemorative Award, which is given by Yeshiva University of New York.

Although Lee was thirty-one and Yang just thirty-five when they received the Nobel Prize in physics, other scientists were not particularly surprised at the youth of the winners. A large majority of the physicists who have received past Nobel Prizes won them for work they did before they were thirty-five years old. (About 30 per cent of them won Nobel Prizes for work done before they were thirty!) The reason for this may be that, in recent years, outstanding achievements in physics have come from brilliant inspirations rather than from collections of data that take a lifetime.

More curious than their youth is the fact that Lee

and Yang were the first scientist-winners of the Nobel Prize to come from China. There has been no Chinese Einstein or Fermi; in pre-Nobel times, there was no Chinese Galileo or Newton.

The Chinese have long preferred painting, writing, and philosophy to science, choosing passive contemplation over active experimentation. And the Chinese people, by and large, were still rather indifferent to science when Lee and Yang were boys. Do-it-yourself projects, for instance, never became at all popular in China; and Frank Yang, who as a boy subscribed to a magazine something like *Popular Mechanics,* had a hard time finding materials for some of the things he wanted to build. There were no lumber yards for two-by-four's and plywood, few books that explained how to build things, and since parents were not in sympathy with such projects, they did not provide advice and the necessary loans of money.

Once Yang and a friend of his designed a motion-picture projector, but they could not find the tools they needed or a shop to work in, so they had to give up the idea. They settled for building a still projector and, Yang says, they did manage to produce quite a few of those.

Today the affable Dr. Yang is impressed by the opportunities young people in the United States have to do-it-themselves. "When you work with your hands," he says, "you learn an attitude about doing things that is just as important as learning skills."

Frank Yang was seven years old when his family

moved to Peiping, a large city in northern China. In Peiping, Frank—who was born, in 1922, in the small town of Hofei, Anhwei province—led a life that was very different from the lives of most Chinese. A vast majority of the Chinese people were on the brink of starvation at that time, and battles between war lords were violent and frequent. Famine and fighting in the streets were a part of everyday life for most of the people in Peiping.

Frank Yang grew up literally outside all of this. His home and the school he went to were built on the campus of Tsinghua University, which was located outside the city walls. Ko-Chuan Yang, his father, was a professor of mathematics at the university; and the Yang children, like the other children of professors, grew up and were educated on the peaceful, isolated campus. There the problems they encountered concerned philosophy, mathematics, or literature, not how to stay alive.

In China, most scholars come from a long line of ancestors who were also scholars. Frank Yang does not know whether this is true of his family, too, because all traces of his ancestors were lost in the middle of the nineteenth century. At that time there was a vast rebellion against the Manchus, the royal dynasty that then ruled China; and in some regions as many as half the inhabitants were killed. Frank's great-grandfather was the only member of the family who escaped from their village, where the fighting was violent.

During his first year in Peiping, Frank discovered mathematics. He was seven years old then, the eldest of the five Yang children, and his father would often talk to him about scientific problems. When the boy found out how interesting science can be, he began to read about it on his own. Partly because of his father's influence, he was most interested in mathematics and thought he would become a mathematician. It was not until he was ready to enter college that Frank changed his mind. He was then studying physics to prepare for a college-entrance exam. While cramming, he discovered that he liked physics better than mathematics and decided to become a physicist.

When Frank Yang was fifteen, the Japanese invaded northern China, and soon Peiping, which is near the northern coast, was threatened. The university that was the Yangs' home, as well as their source of income, was moved to the distant and more secure city of Kunming, in southwestern China. The Yang family moved too, traveling the length of China to reach Kunming. There Tsinghua University and two other large Chinese universities, which also had been moved to Kunming to escape the Japanese, joined together under one name, the National Southwest Associated University. Frank's father resumed his teaching at the newly formed university and Frank studied there.

The Japanese army never reached Kunming, but the city was bombed many times. At the university, classrooms were destroyed, and the campus was pocked with bomb craters. One bomb landed squarely in the courtyard of the Yangs' home. The house was destroyed but, fortunately, every member of the family was away at that moment, and so no one was harmed.

Another physics student at the association of universities in Kunming was the shy, reserved T. D. Lee, who was later to become Frank Yang's friend and collaborator. Lee had also been driven to Kunming by the Japanese invasion.

Though T. D., like Frank, came from a relatively well-off family, he had been more exposed to the chaos of China in the nineteen thirties and forties. He was born in Shanghai, in 1926, the third of six children, only one of them a girl. His father, Tsing-Kong Lee, was a businessman; and so T. D. did not grow up in a cloistered campus atmosphere. He remembers, for instance, a school he attended, in the province of Kiangsi, where, because of the war, there were no teachers. In spite of this, the students showed up in class every day and studied by themselves. "We were each of us his own master," Lee observes.

Lee also recalls that when he was a boy he was an avid reader of stories, in serial form, which were rather a cross between Superman and Robin Hood. The heroes of these stories had magical powers and stole from the rich in order to give to the poor. Their imaginary escapades were based on some fairly recent Chinese history, the underground activity of powerful revolutionary groups, which fought against the Manchu Dynasty and later supported the government of Chiang Kai-shek.

T. D. Lee still likes to read for relaxation and often picks up a mystery story. "When it's a good one," he says, "I can't tell who did it." He also likes to listen to music "if it isn't too noisy."

Like Frank Yang, T. D. read books about science when he was a boy and decided to become a physicist when he entered college. This decision, he says, was based only on his aptitude and interest; nothing else and no one else influenced him.

Up until the time Lee and Yang entered the university at Kunming, their lives had been quite different. But from then on, their paths cross and merge and, in some ways, their lives are almost symmetrical. For instance, both men are married now to young Chinese women whom they met in the United States. (Lee's wife's maiden name was Hui-Chung Chin.) Mrs. Yang and Mrs. Lee both majored in English literature when they were in college, and both the Lees and the Yangs now have two sons each.

Yang and Lee did not know each other when they were in college in Kunming. In 1945, Frank Yang received a fellowship, a sum of money that made it possible for him to go to the United States to continue his studies. The next year Lee also received a fellowship for the same purpose. Both young men chose to go to the University of Chicago, and it was there that they first met. Lee, who seems to like to rove around more than Yang, was thinking about moving on to the University of Michigan when he met Yang. Partly because of this meeting, Lee changed his mind and, like Yang, spent four years in and around the University of Chicago. It made life simpler and happier for both men to be near someone who came from the same country, spoke the same language, and was working in the same field.

During their Chicago years, Lee and Yang began the talks and arguments that culminated in their work on the conservation of parity law. As a result of their talks, they learned one another's language—not Chinese or English but the language of physics. Each one grew to understand how the other approached a problem and what he meant by the words he used. They learned each other's "styles."

Style is as important to a physicist as it is to an artist. In Lee's words, "Each physicist's approach, or style, is different, just as each artist's is. It is possible— it happens quite often in fact—that a style is clumsy and poor but the conclusion is correct."

Lee and Yang have been praised by other scientists for the elegance of their styles. This means that they have taken the best possible routes to reach a goal and have explored these routes, or proofs, neatly, brilliantly, and without wasted effort.

One of the most renowned professors Lee and Yang studied under at the University of Chicago was Enrico Fermi. The two students liked and admired Fermi, for his strong character and integrity as well as for his work. (There are only two pictures on the walls of Yang's office today, one of Einstein and one of Fermi.)

Some time after Fermi's two Chinese students had left the University of Chicago, they helped solve a thorny problem that their professor had raised.

A quarter of a century ago, Enrico Fermi gave the first general description of the weak interactions involved in the nuclear process called beta decay. Little laboratory research on the weak interactions had been done at that time and not much was known about them. Fermi based his description on mathematics and a kind of intuition; he also indicated the complex problem that had to be solved before these weak interactions could be described precisely. For twenty years, numerous experiments were performed in an effort to solve this problem and arrive at an exact understanding of beta decay. But even though the experiments became more and more ingenious and precise as time went on, no solution to the problem was found. Then came Lee and Yang's proposal that parity might not be conserved in the weak interactions. When this was proved to be the case, it opened up a vast, unsuspected area for exploration. There followed an intense investigation of the weak interactions, particularly beta decay; and at last Fermi's problem was solved. As it turned out, and this surprised many physicists, Fermi's twenty-five-year-old description of beta decay corresponded closely to laboratory observations.

Lee and Yang both received their Ph.D.'s while they were at the University of Chicago. After becoming a doctor of physics, Frank Yang taught for a year at the university, and T. D. Lee specialized for a while in astrophysics, the physics of heavenly bodies, doing research at the Yerkes Astronomical Observatory in Wissonsin. Then the roving Lee went out to the West Coast, where he taught and did more research at the University of California, in Berkeley.

In 1951 the two men were reunited at the Institute for Advanced Study, in Princeton, New Jersey. The Institute—IAS for short—is a peaceful place in the country where men of great intellect are paid to think about whatever interests them most. No one checks up on these men, "members" is their official title, no one has anything to say about what they should work on or how they should go about it. The great physicist Robert Oppenheimer is the director of the IAS, but he is there only as a consultant and to see that things run smoothly and informally.

When one of the members—he may be an archeologist, a historian, a mathematician, or a physicist—reaches a point in his work where he feels he has something worth communicating, he has a notice posted on the bulletin board and then gives an informal talk. That is as close as any of the members ever come to teaching, for the purpose of the IAS is to make it possible for members to put all their energy and time into their work, eliminating the necessity to teach—the way most scholars keep themselves and their families alive.

The Institute for Advanced Study is supported by a private grant of five million dollars, rather a lavish investment but, if the history of science is any indication, a sound one. Electricity, the X-ray, the theories of dynamics that are fundamental to industrialized civilization—all are the results of pure, impractical, non-applied research. The men who made these discoveries did not intend to produce something useful; they only wanted more knowledge.

Today there are about one hundred scientists and scholars at the IAS. Some are just visiting for a year or so; others, like Frank Yang, are permanent members and may stay on as long as they wish. Many of the men who are being paid for their "pure" thought are young, good physical specimens, and active, perhaps even *too* active; for along with the few lecture announcements on the bulletin board at the Institute, there is another message, from the Princeton chief of police. In a dignified but firm way, members are warned to watch their driving speed at the foot of a certain hill near the Institute. If they *continue* to exceed the speed limit, says the Chief of Police, it will be necessary to set up a speed trap.

Frank Yang, who now has the title of "professor" at the Institute, inhabits a sunny corner room in this ultimate of ivory towers. Here, on a spring day, he might look out of his window and see a few members conversing together as they stroll across the wide green lawns, other members tossing a plastic plate back and forth and, in the distance, a grazing horse.

Yang's office is quite simple: a desk, a bookcase, a

few chairs, a table, and on it copies of *The New Yorker* magazine. Here he works whenever he is not in New York City, only about an hour away by train. He still goes there often to see T. D. Lee, who has now moved on to Columbia University, where he is the youngest man in recent times to become a full professor.

Although Frank Yang works in an ivory tower, he is not really remote from the world or the people in it. One day, for example, some high school students from a neighboring town called him up with a request. They wanted to know if he would be willing to meet with them regularly and teach them—fill them in, so to speak —on some physics that was more advanced than what they were being taught in school.

Yang readily agreed. He met with the boys regularly for a while and found them bright and interesting. There was one thing about their attitude, though, that bothered him, and still does. Although the boys were curious and eager to learn about things that had a practical application or that could be built, they were not interested in the "pure rules" of physics. Their attitude was: Why bother with abstract knowledge? It's too hard and, anyway, there are exciting practical things we could learn instead.

This attitude toward science, which Yang believes is widespread in America, is just the opposite of the one in China. There people downgrade practical, applied science, work-with-the-hands. They have a don't-do-it-yourself philosophy. Here in America it seems to be theoretical science, work-with-the-mind-alone, that is considered less important. Frank Yang believes that a combination of these two attitudes would be healthier.

In America, he thinks, young people are given freedom to work on whatever appeals to them most. This could be bad, he feels, if the student always avoids what appears to be drudgery.

"It's not enough to have just a burning interest and curiosity," says Frank Yang. "You must also sit down and try to learn the rules of the game; for unless you are immersed in the necessary mental discipline, you cannot *do* anything."

On a May morning in 1956 Lee and Yang began to do something about the conservation of parity law, one of the foundations of physics. This law stems from the principle that the right and left sides of natural forms cannot be distinguished from one another, that they are always symmetrical. Left and right are easy to tell apart in daily life, of course; and some things—for instance, the human being with his heart on the left side—do not appear to be symmetrical at all. But a circumstance like this one does not contradict the principle of right-left symmetry, because physicists are concerned with the way things function. They can imagine humans whose hearts are on the right; and these people, say the physicists, would function just as well as we do. The fact that our hearts *are* on the left is just an accident of environment; it is not evidence of a fundamental lack of symmetry, or asymmetry as it is called.

And so, until early in 1957, physicists were quite sure that the subject matter they studied was always, in essence, symmetrical; and they called the law that was derived from this principle "the conservation of parity law." When Lee and Yang "broke" this law, they released physicists from a straitjacket of ideas that had been shackling them for some time. A new freedom of speculation was the result. Out of it may come a theory that will unify into a meaningful pattern the separate bits of information about our universe that scientists now possess. This theory would account for the constitution and structure of the universe, linking together the cosmos of particles within the atom and the bodies of outer space.

When two physicists set out to topple a fundamental law of their science, what do they do? How do they go about it? The picture that first comes to mind is dramatic and solemn: two white-coated scientists in a vast and spotless laboratory operate miles of intricate apparatus, apparatus that looks as if Dr. Seuss himself had conceived it. The imaginary scientists concentrate on complex experiments and computations, speaking seldom and then only in the form of equations. Their faces express confidence and dedication. Their voices are never raised in laughter, frustration, or argument. Like comic strip characters, they never age. Like mechanical men, they tirelessly follow a rigid, unending routine.

This picture is wrong on almost every count. Tsung Dao Lee and Chen Ning Yang completed the major part of their work in one month. They used no instrument, apparatus, or tool, unless you count paper and pencils. They first went to work on the parity-conservation law in a Chinese restaurant in New York City, where they were having a cup of tea. After that, they worked wherever they happened to be: at home or in the office, strolling on a lawn or riding in a subway.

The two physicists were often on the telephone. During their long conversations, they compared notes, checked on rumors, and argued. They also argued when they got together to talk over their work. The people who overheard these arguments said that they were loud, *very* loud.

Perhaps the most striking difference between a mental picture of Yang and Lee at work and the real thing is the way these two men look.

They appear to be even younger than they are and could easily be mistaken for seniors in high school. Lee, sometimes to the confusion of his professor colleagues, could probably pass as a fifteen-year-old.

When Lee and Yang stopped in at a Chinese restaurant one day early in May, 1956, they had no idea that, before they left, they would reach one of the most important decisions of their lives, a decision that would have a profound and unsettling effect on the science of physics. The two men had gone into the restaurant just to have a cup of tea while they waited for a parking space to become vacant for Yang's car. Yang had driven into New York City that day from Brookhaven National Laboratory, in Long Island. As usual, he had had trouble finding a place to park in the city and had left his car in front of the restaurant for the time being.

As Lee and Yang sipped their tea, they talked about a problem that had been baffling physicists all over the world for some time, a problem they called "the tau-theta puzzle."

During the years since World War II, powerful accelerators have been developed that can break up the atomic nucleus and release the particles that compose it, making it possible to study the nucleus in greater detail than ever before. These accelerators, along with cosmic ray research, have revealed a new world of elementary particles inside the nucleus. Some of these particles provide the force that holds the nucleus together and explain why matter is stable.

Up until 1937 physicists thought that there were only four kinds of particles inside the atom: the electron, the proton, the positron, and the neutron. But to their surprise they continued to discover elementary particles until, at length, they were confronted with a total of about thirty. What is the reason for so many kinds of particles? they asked themselves. What is the purpose of each one? Physicists were *so* puzzled by their new discoveries that they began to call them the "strange" particles. Tau and theta are two of the strange particles that did not behave according to the scientific rules known in 1956.

Tau and theta, which are named after two letters in the Greek alphabet, were found to be identical to each other in every way but one. Their mass, their charge, their length of life were the same; only their parity was different. Parity, a mathematical concept, is always either odd or even. According to the conservation of parity law, a particle could have one parity or the other; it could *never* have both. Therefore tau and theta had to be two different particles, although all other evidence pointed to their being one and the same.

Physicists were far from content with this conclusion. Why, they wondered, should there be two particles that are identical twins in every property but one, their parity? Such a phenomenon had never been observed before. The physicists questioned the accuracy of the research that had shown tau and theta to be almost the same. A few of them even wondered whether the tau-theta puzzle pointed to a flaw in the conservation of parity law. But none of them was able to solve the puzzle.

As Frank Yang put it, someone who was trying to solve the problem of tau and theta was like "a man in a dark room groping for an outlet. He is aware of the fact that in some direction there must be a door that can lead him out of his predicament. But in which direction?" Countless experiments had demonstrated that the parity law was valid. It was founded on what was thought to be a basic, inviolable principle. On the other hand, the laboratory research on tau and theta was quite precise. There was good reason to believe that their properties had been measured accurately.

It made more sense, most physicists felt, to question the research on tau and theta than to question such a fundamental law of physics. After all, the strange particles were recent discoveries and they were not fully understood. But the conservation of parity law was thirty years old and had proved adequate in experiment after experiment.

In science, however, a law is only considered worth preserving when it works. And the more Dr. Lee and Dr. Yang thought about the tau-theta puzzle, the more convinced they became that the laboratory research on the two particles was accurate and could be trusted, and it was the parity law that might be at fault.

As the two scientists sipped their tea that May afternoon, they made their decision, a bold one. They would go to work on the parity-conservation law itself to see if it held true for a group of forces called the "weak interactions," a group to which tau and theta belong because of their rate of disintegration.

Tau and theta disintegrate—or decay, as it is called in physics—at a relatively slow rate. "Relatively" is an important word in the foregoing sentence; actually the decay of tau and theta occurs within about a hundred-millionth of a second (their tracks can be seen in photographs). But a hundred-millionth of a second is a very long time in nuclear reactions, and since a slow decay could be caused only by a weak force, decays like those of tau and theta are called "weak interactions."

Before they left the restaurant, Lee and Yang had agreed to look up the past experiments that had been done on weak interactions to see if there *was* any proof that the parity law held true in this realm of subtle forces.

Soon Dr. Lee and Dr. Yang went their separate ways: Lee to Columbia, where he was a professor; Yang back to Brookhaven National Laboratory, where he was spending the summer with a huge accelerator, the Cosmotron; and the two scientists went to work.

In their case, "work" mostly means thinking, and this thinking is a continuous process. It does not necessarily stop when one of the men leaves his office. T. D. Lee, for instance, may cross the Columbia campus, proceed to walk along Broadway, and enter the subway, without much awareness of his surroundings. In like fashion, during May Frank Yang's mind might have been busy with data on weak interactions while he was brushing his teeth.

"Have you brushed your teeth lately?" one of Yang's friends always asks when they get together. By this, the friend means, "What ideas have you had?"

because once while they were working together, Yang remarked, "When I was brushing my teeth this morning, something occurred to me."

All during the month of May, Lee and Yang studied experiments and thought about the evidence for parity conservation in weak interactions. When one of the scientists hit on something that looked especially interesting, he would phone the other, and they would talk it over. They also continued to meet regularly, often in Chinese restaurants, where the reserved T. D. Lee, who is extremely fond of good food, likes to combine an exchange of ideas with the consumption of a good oriental lunch.

Lee and Yang would often argue about their work during these meetings, but although they were excited and spoke very loudly, their arguments were impersonal. The young men had discovered ten years ago, when they first began talking seriously together, that they learned a lot from arguing with each other. Because of their different backgrounds and temperaments, they would naturally emphasize different aspects of a problem (as any two physicists or, indeed, any two people, would). New points, they found, would be brought out as they argued; and they would both end up with a deeper insight into the matter at hand. Frank Yang puts it in a few words: "As the result of an argument, we would see more than twice each approach."

Sometimes, just for the sake of an argument, Lee and Yang would take stands they did not really believe in. It was fun to argue, they discovered, especially because they were disagreeing about concrete matters. Sooner or later an experiment or a discovery would prove Lee's stand correct and Yang's false, or the other way around; and the argument would be settled.

Another reason why Lee and Yang like to argue may be their temperaments. Neither one could be called a calm person, and when they are both doing what they like best—thinking through a problem, evolving a theory—they probably become intensely excited. It is natural that this excitement would take the form of arguments.

But Lee and Yang do not always get excited and argue when they get together to talk things over. Sometimes they might even tell a joke. One of Frank Yang's favorite stories illustrates the frustrations a physicist is likely to feel when he goes to a mathematician for help with a problem. A mathematician is not interested in using numbers to find an answer to a particular problem; he is interested in numbers for their own sake, as abstractions. A physicist, on the other hand, works with concrete problems about the real world. When he goes to a mathematician, it is because he wants help with the arithmetic for a real, a definite, problem, a problem that he wants *answered.*

Yang's story is about a man with a large bundle of dirty clothes (who symbolizes the physicist with his problem). This man is looking all around for a laundry, but can't find one. Finally, down a back street, he spots a sign on a door, "Laundry Done Here"; so he takes his laundry inside and dumps it on the counter. "I'd like this washed and ironed," he says.

But the man behind the counter (who represents the mathematician) stares at the bundle of laundry as if he'd never seen one before, and then looks questioningly at the man who brought it in.

"This is a laundry, isn't it?" says the man with the bundle.

"No," comes the answer from behind the counter. "We make signs here!"

When physicists come together, even their jokes are likely to be about physics, and Dr. Yang's wife (the former Chih Li Tu) remembers this when she plans a party. She will invite mathematicians and historians and sociologists to an evening get-together, but she hesitates to ask physicists, for fear the party will split down the middle, the ladies on one side of the room and the physicists, deep in talk about their work, on the other.

If Lee and Yang had gone to the same party during the spring of 1956, they probably would have ended up in a corner, arguing about the evidence for parity conservation in weak interactions. The two physicists had started to work on this problem just because they wanted an answer to a question, an answer that might solve the tau-theta puzzle. But as they looked into one piece of research after another, they began to realize the implications of their question. Before the end of the month of May, they had reached a conclusion that, to put it mildly, startled them: there was no evidence whatsoever that parity was conserved in weak interactions.

It was astonishing that scientists had assumed that a law held true when there was no experimental evidence to support that assumption! Even more astonishing was the possibility of a realm that did not behave according to the principle of right-left symmetry, the principle on which the law of parity conservation is founded.

If a sign with a word written on it—the word *pop,* for instance—is held up before a mirror, the reflection of the word looks like:

qOq

because right and left have been reversed. The letter *O* appears the same, because *O* happens to be symmetrical.

Physicists had been sure that all natural forms were essentially like the letter *O,* in that they were symmetrical. That is why they believed that it was impossible to distinguish the mirror image of something they were studying from the real thing.

Now Lee and Yang saw the possibility of a world of nuclear reactions that behaved more like the letter *P;* for no matter how *P* is twisted and turned before a mirror, it is always possible to tell which is the *P* itself and which is its reflection.

Although Lee and Yang were stunned at the *pos·*

sibility of an unsuspected, asymmetrical world, they did not think that such a state of affairs was likely. They doubted, in other words, that the parity-conservation law would prove faulty when it was put to a test. Except in the realm of weak interactions, this law had always held true. It was highly probable that parity would also be conserved in the realm of weak interactions. But there was only one way to find out for sure and that was to experiment.

So Lee and Yang sat down together and planned several intricate experiments. Any one of these would be a decisive test of the parity law, and the fundamental principle of all the experiments was the same: first one of the weak interactions is selected for investigation. Then the weak interaction is studied in two experiments, which are so arranged that they are mirror images of each other. Each experiment has a meter, or counter, to record the final results. If the two meter readings are found to be different, then it has been proved that right-left symmetry, and the parity law derived from this idea, do not hold true.

Lee and Yang wrote up their suggestions for experiments, and their article was circulated among physicists and published by a scientific journal. Then the two young men had to wait until an experimental physicist took up their challenge and actually performed one of the experiments.

Why, one might ask, didn't Lee and Yang do the experiments themselves? The answer is that they are theoretical physicists and are not necessarily suited to laboratory work, a separate science and a very elaborate one, requiring a particular kind of skill and temperament. Both men have studied experimental physics—their work would be badly crippled if they did not have this knowledge—and Yang once spent a year and a half in a laboratory at the University of Chicago. "There," says the outspoken Frank Yang, "I learned a great deal that is important, but I also learned a fact of life: I wouldn't be any good as an experimental man! It requires patience and skill. A piece of equipment may not work, for instance, and the whole experiment must be put to one side until the equipment is fixed. When something like that happens, I tend to get exasperated!"

Yang does not steer clear of the laboratory, however. He believes that it is essential for a theoretical scientist like himself to have some contact with experimental groups. That is why he spends the summer at Brookhaven National Laboratory, studying the "strange" particles produced by the enormous accelerator there.

When Lee and Yang made known their suspicions of the parity law, they offered experimentalists a great opportunity. Quite unexpectedly, scientists did not jump at this chance to fill in an important gap in their knowledge. They read Lee and Yang's paper, commented "How interesting," and then went right on with whatever work they were already doing. When Lee or Yang talked about their proposal to an experimental man, the response was likely to be, "But do you really expect a fantastically exciting outcome?" Then Lee or Yang, whichever one it happened to be, would have to admit that he did not expect that. The two physicists believed that one of their experiments should be done. But if they had been asked to make a bet at that time, they would not have bet at all heavily on the upset of the parity law.

At last one scientist, a woman named Chien Shiung Wu, began to work on Lee and Yang's proposal. Despite the small chance of a dramatic outcome, Miss Wu was willing to put aside her other work and devote six months' time to the painstaking preparation of an elaborate experiment. In doing this, to quote Dr. Yang, "She showed the true scientific spirit, which asks only, 'Is this experiment an exploration of a really fundamental question?' and never asks, 'What is the *practical* significance of this experiment?'"

Miss Wu, who was on the faculty of Columbia University, commuted back and forth each week between New York City and Washington, D.C., where, at the National Bureau of Standards, the experiment was done. Together with a research team under Ernest Ambler, she began to prepare the decisive test of parity. Some difficult problems had to be solved because an experiment of this kind had never been done before. For instance, in order to eliminate outside influences, the experimental set-up had to be kept at a temperature close to absolute zero. (*Note:* More details about the experiment can be found in the April, 1957, issue of the magazine *Scientific American*.)

During the six months that Miss Wu and Mr. Ambler were preparing the parity-law test, Lee and Yang were on the phone more often than ever before. Miss Wu would call them to describe the ups and downs of her work, and the two men would also get calls from curious physicists who had heard rumors about the experiment and wanted to check on them.

One day Miss Wu, in Washington, made phone calls to Dr. Lee and Dr. Yang. She had good news. Some preliminary experimental results looked promising, she said; but of course nothing was definite yet. She asked Lee and Yang not to tell anyone else about these promising results, because the news would be sure to spread far and fast among the physicists, and they would lose no time calling up the National Bureau of Standards to find out what was going on there. "We can't drop everything we're doing here," said Miss Wu, "to answer phone calls from physicists and give them news bulletins."

Dr. Lee and Dr. Yang agreed not to give out the news, and they did not. But the next day Frank Yang was amazed when he got another phone call—from across the North American continent. A physicist in California wanted to know more about those promising preliminary results of Miss Wu's. Before Yang could recover enough from his surprise to reply, the man in California began to tell him all about the results, in great detail. Yang listened with keen interest. The physicist in California knew more about the experiment than Yang knew himself.

During the December of 1956, assorted physicists spread around the country ran up rather large phone bills as they tracked down rumors about the upset of parity. When the result of Miss Wu's experiment was at last announced, in January, 1957, the curious physicists received what one commentator called, "a rude but exhilarating shock." For the two very different meter readings revealed what even Lee and Yang had doubted was possible: a weak interaction and its mirror image are not always the same; left can be distinguished from right. The principle of right-left symmetry had collapsed, and with it, the conservation of parity law.

By the time Miss Wu and Mr. Ambler's results were announced, four other groups, in New York, Chicago, Moscow, and Leiden, Holland, had begun to work on similar experiments based on Lee and Yang's proposals. The results of all these experiments confirmed the first one.

When Frank Yang is asked whether he and T. D. Lee celebrated after they heard the good news, he smiles and says, "No. Joy was not paramount in our minds. At that time we felt an intense excitement, because so many questions could now be asked, so many answers were ready to be approached."

During 1957, physicists, including Lee and Yang,

were busy with these questions and answers; and they accumulated a large body of information. Now that they no longer had to make their observations of the weak interactions conform to the parity law, they were more free to speculate and make theories. They became suspicious of the other great conservation laws and wondered whether they, too, would collapse in the realm of subtle interactions.

One physicist, Philip Morrison, writing in *Scientific American,* wondered if the law of energy conservation would still hold "for the weakest interactions of all, those involving the weak force of gravity. Here," he went on, "one thinks of the hypothesis that matter may arise spontaneously from a space containing no energy, and the possibilities are exciting."

Physicists are also speculating about a connection between the absence of symmetry in weak interactions and the near absence of anti-matter (particles that, except for their opposite charge, are twins of other elementary particles) in our world. These two major asymmetries may point toward a larger symmetry, involving a universe of anti-matter with an asymmetry to balance the asymmetry of our own universe. Here, physicists think, may be a link between the physics of outer space and the physics of elementary particles.

Since winning the Nobel Prize, Lee and Yang have continued to be active and productive in the science of elementary particles, which has come to be known as "particle physics." Out of this new science may come answers to such questions as: What is the purpose of the strange particles and why are there so many of them? What is the meaning of the asymmetry of weak interactions? Do the usual concepts of time and space apply in this realm of weak and elusive forces? Perhaps Lee and Yang will discover the answers to some of these questions.

But the two young theoreticians do not always stay within the bounds of particle physics. When they hear about a new problem that sounds interesting, they go to work on it, whether it concerns astrophysics, field theory, or statistical mechanics. Few other men are able to rove over the entire subject matter of physics in this way; for an exceptionally high level of intelligence and energy are required.

In addition to their brains and energy, Lee and Yang have something else in their favor—the fact that they work together. Two minds are better than one, and two minds that understand each other and that can work on the same high level are best of all. As Lee and Yang analyze problems and clash in argument together, sparks are given off, sparks that light up new areas of knowledge.

INDEX

315